Greeting Cards

By Murray Suid

Illustrated by Lisa Levine

This book is for Allison, Deann, and Win Kato

Publisher: Roberta Suid
Editor: Mary McClellan
Design: David Hale
Production: Susan Pinkerton

Other books by the author: *Book Factory, Editing, Letter Writing, Research, Sentences, Speaking and Listening, Stories, Words, Writing Hangups.*

Entire contents copyright © 1988 by Monday Morning Books, Inc., Box 1680, Palo Alto, California 94302

Monday Morning is a registered trademark of Monday Morning Books, Inc.

ISBN 0-912107-74-X

Printed in the United States of America
9 8 7 6 5 4 3 2 1

CONTENTS

INTRODUCTION

Roses are red.
Violets are blue.
For art fun and writing
It's greeting cards and you.

If you want kids to have a real reason for writing, this is the book for you. *Greeting Cards* offers dozens of projects where words genuinely matter. Children will learn how to combine pictures and sentences in order to do everything from giving thanks to saying "Please get well."

While delighting their readers, young card makers will sharpen a wide variety of thinking and writing skills. These include describing, rhyming, defining, creating dialogue, captioning pictures, labeling maps, and using lettering to emphasize an idea.

WHAT YOU'LL NEED

This book might be called *The Recyclery*. Most of the projects require only cheap or free "found" materials—pictures clipped from magazines and newspapers, yarn, foil, buttons, and labels, plus the kind of stuff you find at the bottom of overfilled desk drawers.

Of course, you'll also be using some standard craft items, such as glue, tape, staples, stick-on stars, glitter, crayons, and colored construction paper. The term "writing tools" refers to things like crayons and felt-tip pens.

One of the key materials is scratch paper for making rough drafts of the text that will appear on the cards. By refining their thoughts, children will get important practice in the vital composition skill of editing.

The Resources section of this book provides a simple guide to basic card construction: for example, ways to make multi-sided cards. Also, you will find a calendar of often-overlooked celebrations—for example, Good Neighbor Day—to inspire card making on any day of the year. Finally, there are pages of copy art, drawing tips, lettering techniques, and a rhyming dictionary.

HOW NOT TO RUN OUT OF IDEAS

Greeting Cards is organized alphabetically by type of card, from all-purpose to valentine. As you flip through the book, you'll notice more than a dozen familiar formats, such as "see-through" and "sing-along" cards. Each type of card can be used in many ways. (See Quick Guide to Formats below.) For example, kids can turn the invitation calendar card into a congratulations note or into a birth announcement card. All you'll need to do is add a little imagination. Luckily, that's one ingredient that is free and that is never in short supply. In fact, the more kids use it, the more there is to use. Hmm. Maybe there ought to be a National Imagination Week!

Quick Guide to Formats

Format	Section
Acrostic	Friendship
Balloon	Congratulations
Calendar	Invitation
Cartoon	Parent's Day
Certificate	Parent's Day
Checklist	All-Purpose, Thank You
Clock	Invitation
Collage	Parent's Day
Dot-to-Dot	Thank You
Egg	Easter
Glue-On	Chanukah, Get Well
Headline	Invitation
Jigsaw	Congratulations
Map	Bon Voyage, Invitation
Mask	Halloween
Mirror	Valentine
Object	Birthday, Book Report
Ornament	Christmas
Place Card	Thanksgiving
Pull-Up	Christmas
Quiz	Graduation
Rebus	Valentine
Rhyme	Birthday
Secret Message	Valentine
See-Through	Birthday, Invitation
Shape	Birthday, Christmas
Spinner	Birthday
Ticket	Birth Announcement

ALL-PURPOSE CARD

MATERIALS: paper, writing tools

DIRECTIONS:
1. Fold a piece of paper to make a card.
2. At the top of the card, write something like: I know I owe you a card for something.
3. Under the headline, list several greetings such as: Happy Birthday, Happy New Year, and Get Well. Put a check box in front of each one.
4. Next, write something like: Please check the right box.
5. Inside the card, write a message about the real reason for the card.

Message inside

I know I owe you a card for something:
☐ Happy Birthday
☐ Get Well
☐ Have a Good Trip
☐ Thank You
☐ Be My Valentine

Please check the right box!

ANNIVERSARY QUOTATION CARD

MATERIALS: paper, writing tools, quotation book

DIRECTIONS:
1. Fold a piece of paper to make a card.
2. Find a quotation that fits the people who are having the anniversary. The quotation might come from a poem or a song.
3. At the top of the card, write something like: Happy 20th Anniversary.
4. Under the headline, write the quotation and who said it.
5. Draw a picture that goes with the quotation.
6. Inside the card, write an anniversary message.

Message inside

BIRTH ANNOUNCEMENT TICKET

MATERIALS: paper, writing tools, index card, drawing or photograph

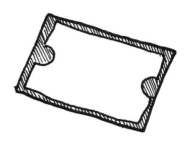

DIRECTIONS:
1. Cut out an index-size card.
2. Label the card "Admit one."
3. Explain that the ticket will allow the person to see the newborn.
4. Give information about visiting hours.
5. On the back of the card, tell about the newborn. Add a drawing or photograph.

Variation: Use the same idea to make an invitation.

BIRTHDAY CANDLE CARD

MATERIALS: paper, writing tools, yellow crayon

DIRECTIONS:
1. Draw a large candle with a flame and then cut it out.
2. Color the flame yellow.
3. Print the birthday person's age on the flame.
4. Write a birthday message on the candle.

Variation: Use the same idea to make an anniversary card.

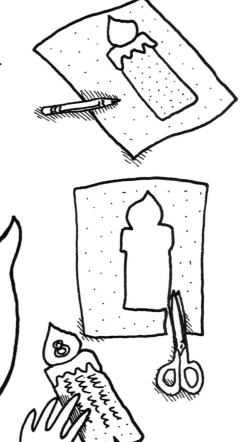

Happy Birthday Sally
I hope this year is
as bright as this candle.
Your friend, Nancy

BIRTHDAY GIFT MACHINE CARD

MATERIALS: paper, writing tools, plastic bag, tape, nuts, bolts, wire, and other stuff

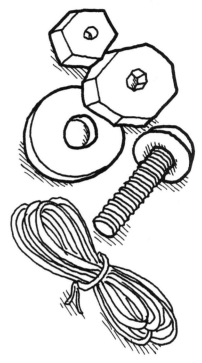

DIRECTIONS:
1. Cut out a two-sided card.
2. Draw a picture of a crazy-looking machine. Cut it out.
3. Put some nuts, bolts, wire, or other stuff in a plastic bag.
4. Tape the bag and the picture to the card.
5. At the top of the card, print: Gift Machine.
6. At the bottom of the card, write something like: Use the parts in the bag to finish the machine and it will make any gift you want.
7. Write a real birthday message on the other side.

BIRTHDAY MEASURING TAPE CARD

MATERIALS: paper, writing tools, string or yarn, scissors, plastic bag, stapler or tape

DIRECTIONS:
1. Fold a piece of paper to make a card.
2. Cut a piece of string or yarn that's at least a head longer than the birthday person is tall.
3. Put the strip in a plastic bag, and attach the bag to page two of the card.
4. On page one, write a note that explains how the string can be used each year to measure the person's growth. Draw a picture to show how to use the string.
5. Add a birthday message on page three of the card.

Happy Birthday, Tab

Put the loop of this string over your toe, then tie a knot in the string to show how tall you are. Next year, you'll see how much you've grown.

BIRTHDAY NUMBER CARD

MATERIALS: paper, writing tools, newspapers and magazines, scissors, paste

DIRECTIONS:
1. Fold a piece of paper to make a card.
2. On scratch paper, make a list of things that have the same number as the person's birthday. For example, if the person is ten, the list might include ten toes.
3. At the top of the card, write something like: Happy Tenth Birthday. Ten is a great number.
4. Under the headline, list the good things about the number.
5. Draw or use cut-out art to illustrate the number.
6. Inside the card, write a birthday message.

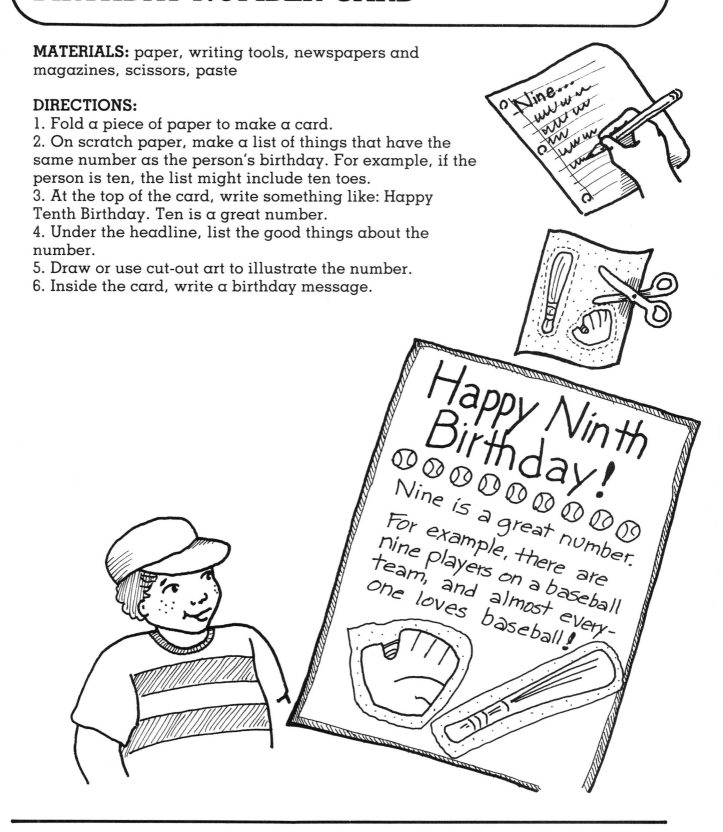

BIRTHDAY SEE-THROUGH CARD

MATERIALS: paper, writing tools, tape or stapler, scissors

DIRECTIONS:
1. Cut out a two-sided card.
2. On scratch paper, write a birthday message.
3. Neatly copy the message onto the card.
4. Along the top edge, tape or staple a piece of thin writing paper so it covers the card. It should be possible to lift the cover sheet.
5. Hold the two sheets up to the light and, with a pencil, lightly mark where a few of the words are.
6. Cut "word windows" in the top sheet. Erase any pencil marks.
7. At the top of this sheet write: Here are a few words for your birthday.

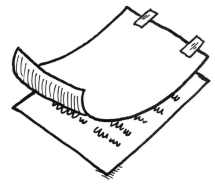

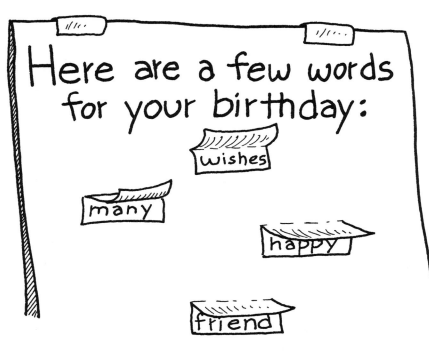

BIRTHDAY WISHING WHEEL

MATERIALS: paper plate, writing tools, ruler, brad, construction paper

DIRECTIONS:
1. With a ruler, draw lines that divide the plate into six pieces, as if it were a pie.
2. In each piece, write a wish that the person getting the card might make. The wishes can be serious or silly.
3. Cut a pointer out of the construction paper.
4. Use the brad to attach the pointer to the plate.
5. Around the edge of the card, tell how the card works. For example: Spin the arrow and get a happy birthday wish.
6. On the back of plate, write a birthday message.

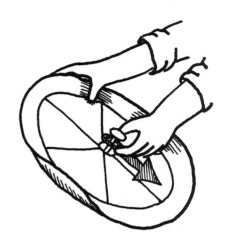

BIRTHDAY YOU-RHYME-IT CARD

MATERIALS: paper, writing tools

DIRECTIONS:
1. Fold a piece of paper to make a card.
2. On a piece of scratch paper, list some rhyming words that might go on a birthday card: for example, gift/lift and older/bolder. If possible, include a rhyme using the birthday person's name: for example, Fred/red.
3. On the card's front, draw someone writing. Then write a headline like: I've started a poem for your birthday.
4. On page two of the card, write: Now all you have to do is finish it.
5. On page three of the card, draw lines for the person to write on. Put a rhyming word at the end of each line.
6. On page four of the card, write a birthday greeting for the person. This greeting can be in rhyme or not.

BON VOYAGE MAP CARD

MATERIALS: paper, writing tools, map of place where the person is going, paste

DIRECTIONS:
1. Fold a piece of paper to make a card.
2. On the card, draw or glue a map of the place where the traveler will visit. Travel agents often will have such maps printed on travel brochures.
3. Add a headline: for example, Have a good time in London.
4. Inside the card, tell the traveler some things to see or do in the place. For ideas, read a book or talk to someone who has been there.

Variation: Write a bon voyage card for an imaginary journey: for example, a trip to Mars or a trip in a time machine.

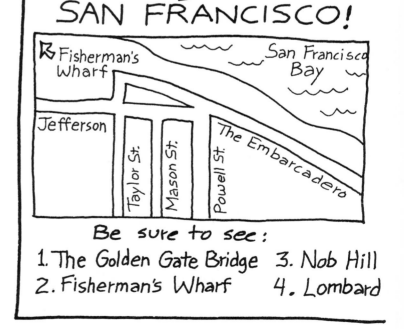

Have a good time in
SAN FRANCISCO!

Fisherman's Wharf · San Francisco Bay · Jefferson · Taylor St. · Mason St. · Powell St. · The Embarcadero

Be sure to see:
1. The Golden Gate Bridge
2. Fisherman's Wharf
3. Nob Hill
4. Lombard

BOOK REPORT CARD

MATERIALS: paper, writing tools, plastic bag, stapler or tape, any small item that could be from a place in the book

DIRECTIONS:
1. Fold a piece of paper to make a card.
2. Find something that represents a place in the book. Some examples: sand from the beach or peanuts from the zoo.
3. Put the object in a plastic bag, and seal the bag.
4. Staple or tape the bag to the front of the card.
5. Above the bag, tell what's in the bag and where it's from.
6. Inside the card, write about the place and the book.

Variation: Write a pretend wish-you-were-here card about an imaginary place: for example, Alice's Wonderland.

Pepper from the Duchess' kitchen

"A-choo!" Wonderland is fun: Greetings from Alice!

Book report goes on back

MENORAH CARD

MATERIALS: paper, writing tools, small plastic bag, peel-off labels

DIRECTIONS:
1. Fold a piece of construction paper.
2. Draw a menorah on the inside two pages. The menorah should have nine candle holders.
3. Using a different color of construction paper, cut out nine candles and glue them to the candle holders.
4. Cut nine candle flames out of the peel-off labels, leaving the backing on.
5. Put the flames in the plastic bag and attach the bag to the front of the card.
6. At the top of side one write: Happy Chanukah.
7. In the space near the bag, write that the flames are to be put on the candles, one at a time until the eighth night.
8. Write a Chanukah message under the menorah or on side four of the card.

CHRISTMAS ELF'S POCKET CARD

MATERIALS: paper, writing tools, scissors, tape

DIRECTIONS:
1. Cut out a two-sided card.
2. Draw an elf.
3. Cut out a pocket.
4. Attach the pocket to the picture by taping it on three sides leaving the top open.
5. Write a Christmas greeting, and put it into the pocket.
6. On the outside of the pocket tell where the note is.

CHRISTMAS ORNAMENT CARD

MATERIALS: paper, writing tools, hole punch, stars, yarn

DIRECTIONS:
1. Think up an ornament for someone's Christmas tree.
2. Cut the ornament from a piece of construction paper.
3. Decorate one side of the ornament using stars or crayons.
4. On the other side of the ornament, write
   Here's a greeting to hang from your Christmas tree.
5. Under those words, write your Christmas message.
6. Punch a hole at the top of the ornament and push a piece of yarn through the hole.

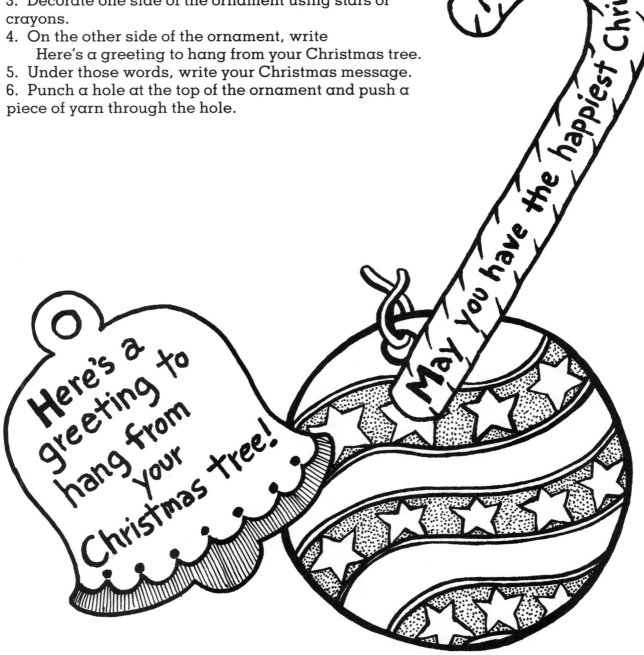

CHRISTMAS PULL-UP CARD

MATERIALS: paper, drawing tools, scissors, stapler

DIRECTIONS:
1. Cut out a two-sided card.
2. On the front of the card, draw a house with a wide chimney. Next to the chimney draw a sleigh with eight reindeer.
3. Cut a slit in the chimney.
4. On a strip of paper narrower than the slit, draw Santa Claus. Print the word "Pull" on Santa's cap.
5. At the bottom of the Santa Claus strip, staple a tab.
6. Slip the Santa through the slit.
7. Write a Christmas message on the back of the card.

Staple tab to bottom of strip

Christmas message on back of card

CONGRATULATIONS BLOW-UP

MATERIALS: paper, writing tools, balloon, felt-tip pen, envelope

DIRECTIONS:
1. On a small piece of paper, write a note congratulating someone for doing something special: for example, singing well in a concert or winning a prize.
2. Roll up the message and slip it into a balloon.
3. Have a helper blow up the balloon and pinch it closed so the air won't leak.
4. With a felt pen print "Congratulations" in big letters on the balloon. In smaller letters, print: Message inside.
5. Let the air out of the balloon.
6. Wash off the tube part of the balloon.
7. Put the balloon in an envelope with a piece of paper that reads: Blow me up.

Note rolled up.

Congratulations Message inside

Have a friend help hold the balloon.

Balloon and message in envelope.

Blow me up!

CONGRATULATIONS PUZZLE

MATERIALS: picture, paper, drawing tools, paste, scissors, plastic bag

DIRECTIONS:
1. Find or draw a picture of something related to the congratulations message. For example, if the person getting the card hit a home run, the picture might be a photo from the sports page.
2. Paste the picture on a card-size piece of paper.
3. Under the picture, write a message.
4. In pencil, lightly trace a jigsaw pattern on the picture so that there will be about six or eight pieces.
5. Cut the pieces out and put them into an envelope.
6. On the envelope, explain how the puzzle card works.

Variation: Use the same idea to make a thinking-of-you card.

Put the pieces together and read the message!

EASTER EGG-CITING MESSAGE

MATERIALS: paper, writing tools, egg, marking pens or crayons, water-based paint

DIRECTIONS:
1. Poke a small hole in each end of the egg.
2. Blow out the yolk, rinse the egg, and let it dry.
3. On a tiny piece of paper, write an Easter greeting.
4. Roll up the message, and put it into the egg.
5. On the outside of the egg, print a note telling the person that there's a message inside.
6. Decorate the egg.

Variation: Leave part of the message sticking out of the egg so the person doesn't have to break the egg to read the note.

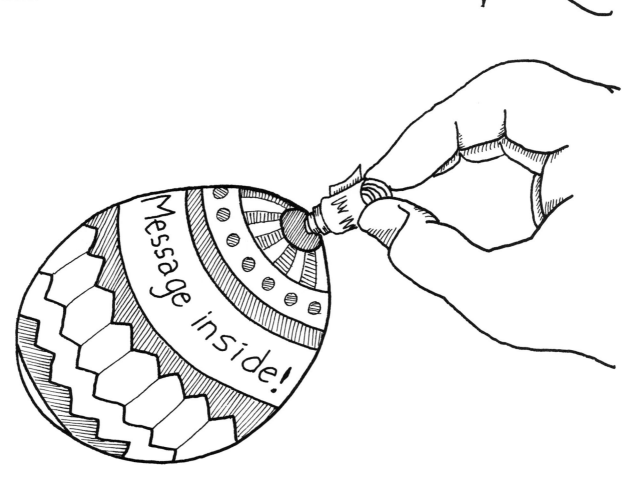

EASTER YOU-COLOR-IT CARD

MATERIALS: paper, writing tools, crayons or colored pencils, plastic bag, tape or stapler

DIRECTIONS:
1. Fold a piece of paper to make a card.
2. On pages two and three, draw an Easter scene that looks like art from a coloring book.
3. Put a few crayons or colored pencils in the plastic bag, and seal the bag.
4. Attach the bag to the front of the card.
5. Write directions for using the crayons to color the card.
6. On the back of the card, write an Easter message.

FRIENDSHIP ACROSTIC NOTE

MATERIALS: paper, writing tools

DIRECTIONS:
1. Fold a piece of paper to make a card.
2. On scratch paper, print the friend's name. Then write a word for each letter. The words should tell about the person.

    T errific
    H elpful
    E nergetic
    O utstanding

3. On the card itself, leave a blank for each letter that starts the name but fill in the rest of each word.

    __ errific
    __ elpful
    __ nergetic
    __ utstanding

4. At the top of the card, ask the person to fill in the letters.
5. Add a picture that shows something about the person.
6. Inside the card, write a friendly message.

Variation: Make an acrostic thank-you note. Use the name of the gift as the starting word.

A... artistic!

Complete the words and you'll spell the name of my best friend!

__ eace-loving
__ rtistic
__ nderstanding
__ ively
__ lways helpful

friendly message inside

FRIENDSHIP MISS YOU CARD

MATERIALS: paper, writing tools, glue or tape,
photograph of person receiving the card

DIRECTIONS:
1. Before taking a trip, get a photograph of the person who
will be receiving the card.
2. During the trip, buy a postcard or take a photograph of
an important scene on the trip: for example, a famous
landmark or the beach.
3. Tape the photo of the person who will receive the card
onto the photograph.
4. Attach the photograph to a piece of construction paper.
5. Above the photograph write: Wish you were here.
6. On the back of the card, tell about the trip and why it
would be nice if the person were along.

FRIENDSHIP PEN PAL NOTE

MATERIALS: paper, writing tools, penny, tape

DIRECTIONS:
1. Fold a piece of paper to make a card.
2. At the top of the first page of the card, print: A _____ for your thoughts.
3. Tape a penny over the blank.
4. On the inside of the card, write a message that asks the pen pal to write a letter that tells what's happening in his or her life.

A ¢ ¢

for your thoughts

Dear Ricky,
It's been a while since I heard from you. How have you been? Did you have a good time on your trip to Niagara Falls? I hope you'll tell me all about it.

FRIENDSHIP SEEDY CARD

MATERIALS: paper, writing tools, fruit or vegetable seed, glue or tape

DIRECTIONS:
1. Fold a piece of paper to make a card.
2. At the top of the card, write a headline like: I hope our friendship grows like a...
3. Paste or tape the seed onto the card.
4. Under the seed, name the plant.
5. On the inside of the card, write a friendly note.

Variation: Make a seedy birthday card that tells the person to grow as fast or as strong or as sweet as the seed.

GET WELL BANDAGE CARD

MATERIALS: paper, writing tools, bandage

DIRECTIONS:
1. Fold a piece of paper to make a card.
2. At the top of the card, write something like: I want you to get well because...
3. In the middle of the card, use a bandage to trace a rectangle.
4. In the rectangle, give the reasons for wanting the person to get well. An example would be: I want to go to the movies with you.
5. Attach the bandage to the card so that it covers the message.
6. On the bandage, print: Pull off!
7. Add a cheerful picture.
8. Write a longer get-well message inside the card.

GET WELL SMILE CARD

MATERIALS: paper, writing tools

DIRECTIONS:
1. Fold a piece of paper to make a card.
2. On the front of the card draw a face that frowns when seen right-side up, but that smiles when turned upside down.
3. At the top of the card, print the words: When you're sick, I look like this.
4. Turn the card upside down and print the words: When you're well, I look like this.
5. Inside the card, write a letter that will cheer up the person.

GRADUATION QUIZ CARD

MATERIALS: paper, writing tools, dictionary

DIRECTIONS:
1. Fold a piece of paper to make a card.
2. Pick out a word that looks as if it would be hard to spell.
3. On the front of the card, write a headline that reads: Check the correct spelling.
4. Under the headline, write the word three times, once correctly and twice incorrectly. Put little boxes in front of each word.
5. At the bottom of the page, write something like: The answer is on page four of this card.
6. On page two of the card, write something like: Are you glad you're finished with spelling tests, at least for a while?
7. On page three, write a congratulations note to the graduate.
8. On page four, write the correct spelling and the meaning of the word.

Variation: Instead of spelling words, use historical facts or a tricky math problem.

Message of congratulations inside

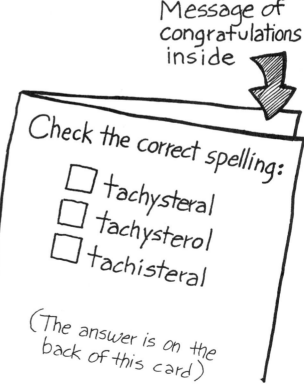

Check the correct spelling:

☐ tachysteral
☐ tachysterol
☐ tachisteral

(The answer is on the back of this card)

Correct answer on back

HALLOWEEN MASK CARD

MATERIALS: paper, writing tools, chalk, scissors, hole punch, hole reinforcements, yarn

DIRECTIONS:
1. Hold the paper to the face and use a piece of chalk to mark gently where the eyes, mouth, and nose belong.
2. Draw a scary face on the paper.
3. Cut out the eyes and mouth.
4. Punch a hole on each side of the mask. Put gummed reinforcements on both sides of the holes.
5. Use the holes to attach a piece of yarn for holding the mask in place.
6. On the reverse side of the mask, write a Halloween greeting. Also give directions for wearing the mask.

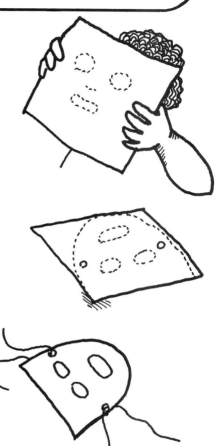

(front)

Here's how to have a scary Halloween:
1. Put on this mask.
2. Stand in front of a mirror.
3. Say "Boo!"

(back)

INVITATION BUILDING CARD

MATERIALS: paper, writing tools, scissors, tape

DIRECTIONS:
1. Cut out a two-sided card.
2. On one side, draw a picture of the building where the party will take place. Be sure to include a large door.
3. Cut a door shape from another piece of paper. Tape the door onto the drawing so that it will swing open.
4. On the outside of the door, write: Open.
5. Open the door and write the invitation message. Tell where and when the party will take place. List some of the activities that are planned.

Variation: Use the same open-it idea for a valentine.

INVITATION CALENDAR CARD

MATERIALS: paper, writing tools

DIRECTIONS:
1. Fold a piece of paper to make a card.
2. Draw a calendar page.
3. Number the days of the month.
4. Circle the day of the party. Write the time of the party in the square.
5. In the picture area, draw a scene from the party.
6. Inside the card, write a note that gives other information about the party.

Variation: Use a calendar to make a bon voyage card, a birthday card, or a graduation card.

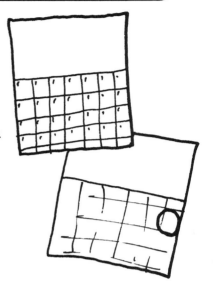

More information about the party inside

INVITATION CLOCK CARD

MATERIALS: paper, writing tools, small plain paper plate with a flat area surrounded by a raised edge

DIRECTIONS:
1. Print 12 numbers around the inner circle of the plate.
2. Draw the hands to the time when the party is to start.
3. On the clock face, print the date.
4. Around the edge of the plate, print the reason for the party and an RSVP message.
5. Print more details on the back of the plate. Or use the back for a picture of some activity that will happen at the party: for example, people playing a game or eating food.

clock

date

message

Picture of game or activity goes on other side

INVITATION HEADLINE CARD

MATERIALS: paper, writing tools, newspapers and magazines, scissors, paste

DIRECTIONS:
1. Fold a piece of paper to make a card.
2. Think up a headline for the card: for example, You're invited to a Surprise Party.
3. Look for newspaper or magazine headlines that contain some of these words.
4. Clip the words and make the headline for the card. Add hand-lettered words if needed.
5. Try to find a picture to illustrate the headline. For example, an advertisement or sports photo might show a person who looks surprised.
6. Inside the card, give information about when and where the party will take place.

INVITATION MAP CARD

MATERIALS: paper, writing tools, map of neighborhood

DIRECTIONS:
1. Fold a piece of paper to make a card.
2. On the front, draw a map of the neighborhood where the party will take place. If needed, use a real map as a model.
3. Circle the place where the party will be held.
4. Inside the card, give facts about the event: what it's about, when it will happen, where it will happen, and so on.
5. For more interest, add pictures on the back.

Come to Room 26's Open House! October 14, 7:15 P.M.

PARK AVE.

MAIN ST.

HAYES SCHOOL

CENTER BLVD.

GREEN ST.

(Front)

See our reading center.

Use our new microscope

Enjoy a funny skit about fitness.

(Back)

INVITATION PLATTER CARD

MATERIALS: paper plate, writing tools, newspapers and magazines, scissors, empty food boxes and labels, paste

DIRECTIONS:
1. Clip small pictures of party food from newspapers, magazines, labels, or packages. Examples include sandwiches, fruit, and cookies.
2. Paste the pictures in the center of the paper plate.
3. Around the edge of the plate, write the invitation message.

NEW YEAR'S RESOLUTIONS CARD

MATERIALS: paper, writing tools, scissors, plastic bag, tape or stapler

DIRECTIONS:
1. Fold a piece of paper to make a card.
2. On another piece of paper, draw a picture of a safe.
3. Cut out the safe and make a slit in it near the top.
4. Tape the safe to the front of the card. Over the safe, write: Keep your New Year's resolutions in here.
5. Put a bunch of tiny slips of paper into the plastic bag.
6. Tape or staple the bag inside the card.
7. Over the bag write: Use paper to write New Year's Resolutions.
8. Inside the card or on the back, write a New Year's message.

41

PARENT'S DAY BABY TALK CARD

MATERIALS: paper, writing tools, baby picture, scissors, glue

DIRECTIONS:
1. Fold a piece of paper to make a card.
2. Get a baby picture from the family photo album, or clip one from a newspaper, magazine, or baby-product box.
3. Attach the picture to the front of the card. Leave room above and below the picture.
4. Draw a dialogue (talk) balloon over the picture.
5. In the balloon, write something like: Happy Mother's Day! or Happy Father's Day!
6. Inside the card, write a Mother's Day or Father's Day message.

Variation: Use the same idea for a grandparent's day card.

PARENT'S DAY CERTIFICATE

MATERIALS: paper, writing tools, foil, glue

DIRECTIONS:
1. On a piece of scratch paper, write something like: This card certifies that my mother (or father) is a terrific parent because _____. Then complete the sentence.
2. Print the words carefully onto a notebook-size piece of paper.
3. Draw a border around the words.
4. Glue on an official-looking seal made from aluminum or gold foil.
5. Sign the card.
6. On the back, write a parent's day message.

Variation: Make certificates for grandparents, aunts, uncles, cousins, friends, or neighbors.

HAPPY MOTHER'S DAY

This card certifies that my mom is a great mom, because she always helps me to do my best. Even when I do something wrong, she has a smile for me.

Julie

PARENT'S DAY COLLAGE

MATERIALS: paper, writing tools, old magazines and newspapers, scissors, paste

DIRECTIONS:
1. Fold a piece of paper to make a card.
2. Find several pictures that show the things a father or mother can do.
3. Paste the pictures onto the front of the card.
4. Write a headline above the pictures.
5. Inside the card, write a parent's day message.

Message to Dad inside

PARENT'S DAY COMICS

MATERIALS: paper, writing tools, newspaper with comics, scissors, paste

DIRECTIONS:
1. Fold a piece of paper to make a card.
2. Clip a comic strip from a newspaper, and paste it to the card.
3. Paste pieces of paper over the dialogue (talk) balloons.
4. Write new words in the balloons.
5. Inside the card, write a longer, more serious message.

ST. PATRICK'S DAY CARD

MATERIALS: paper, writing tools, green pen or crayon, stick-on labels, plastic bag, tape or stapler

DIRECTIONS:
1. Cut out a long, thin card.
2. Write a headline that says something like: Whatever you're wearing on St. Patrick's Day. . .
3. Then list all kinds of clothing.
4. Under the list write: make it green.
5. Color a bunch of stick-on labels green.
6. Put the labels into the plastic bag.
7. Staple or tape the bag to the card.
8. On the back of the card, write a St. Patrick's Day message.

Whatever you're wearing on St. Patrick's Day...
☐ shirt
☐ hat
☐ pants
☐ jacket
☐ shoes

Message on back

make it green!

THANK YOU CHECKLIST

MATERIALS: paper, writing tools

DIRECTIONS:
1. Fold a piece of paper to make a card.
2. At the top of the card, write: Thank you for...
3. List many gifts, including the one that the person really gave. Some might be silly: for example, a dinosaur.
4. In front of each item on the list, put a check box.
5. Now write: I can't wait to...
6. List many activities that can be done with different gifts. Include one that fits the real gift: for example, ride it, eat it, paint it, put it in the freezer, take it apart.
7. Put check boxes in front of each item on the list.
8. Put a check mark next to each box that makes sense.
9. Inside the card, write a serious note that tells why the gift was appreciated.

Thank you for...
☐ the red sports car
☐ the trip to Australia
☐ the cute alligator
☐ the beautiful baseball cap

I can't wait to...
☐ drive it
☐ photograph it
☐ wrestle it
☐ wear it to the next home game.

Message of thanks inside

THANK YOU DOT-TO-DOT

MATERIALS: paper, writing tools

DIRECTIONS:
1. Fold a piece of paper to make a card.
2. Lightly draw a simple outline picture of whatever the thank-you note is about.
3. Make heavy dots at each important point in the drawing. Then erase the outline.
4. Number the dots in the order that would help a person draw the thing.
5. At the top of the card, write something like: Connect the dots to see what's making me happy.
6. Inside the card, write a detailed note that explains how the thing is being used.

Variation: Make a dot-to-dot Halloween card.

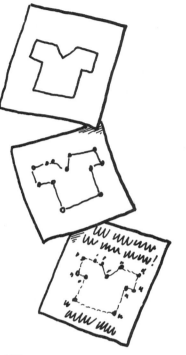

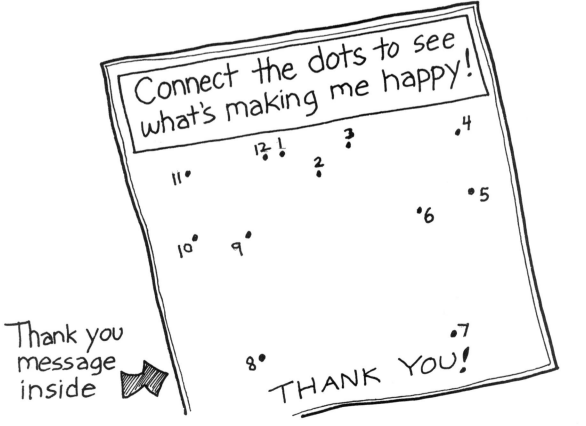

THANKSGIVING PLACE CARDS

MATERIALS: paper, writing tools, magazines and newspapers, scissors, paste

DIRECTIONS:
1. Draw pictures of things to be thankful for, or clip pictures from magazines and newspapers.
2. Fold pieces of construction paper to make displays that stand by themselves.
3. Paste a picture onto each display.
4. Write a line of thanks under each picture: for example, I'm thankful for the sunrise.
5. On the other side, write the name of the person who will sit at that place for dinner.

I'm thankful for the singing birds.

Irwin Hill

VACATION TRAVEL CARD

MATERIALS: paper, writing tools, magazines and newspapers, scissors

DIRECTIONS:
1. Fold a piece of paper to make a card.
2. Draw or find a picture of an airplane, auto, camel, or other way of getting from one place to another.
3. Attach the picture to the front of the card.
4. At the top of the card, write something like: Getting here was half the fun.
5. Inside the card, write about the trip from home to the place being visited. Tell about unusual things that happened or were seen.

Variation: Use the same idea for a book report about a travel adventure book.

What a trip!

News about the trip inside

VALENTINE MIRROR

MATERIALS: paper, writing tools, scissors, aluminum foil, paste or tape

DIRECTIONS:
1. Cut out a heart-shaped card.
2. In the center, paste or tape a piece of aluminum foil to be used as a mirror.
3. Paste or draw a lace border around the mirror.
4. Write a few sentences or a poem telling the person who gets the card why he or she should look in the mirror.

Valentine:
Here's a card with mirror and lace
So you can see your pretty face.

VALENTINE REBUS

MATERIALS: paper, writing tools

DIRECTIONS:
1. Fold a piece of paper to make a card.
2. On scratch paper, create a rebus message for a valentine. A rebus is a phrase or sentence that uses pictures in place of words or parts of words. For example, a drawing of an eye can stand for the word "I."
3. Copy the rebus onto the front of the card.
4. Inside the card, write a valentine letter or poem.

Letter or poem for valentine goes inside

VALENTINE SECRET MESSAGE

MATERIALS: paper, writing tools, carbon paper, scissors, glue

DIRECTIONS:
1. Cut out a card in the shape of a heart.
2. On scratch paper, write a valentine message.
3. At the top of the card, write something like: A secret message for my valentine.
4. Place a piece of writing paper over a piece of carbon paper, with the carbon (ink) side up.
5. Place a second sheet of writing paper on top of the first.
6. Write the message on the top sheet.
7. Remove the top sheet. The message will appear in backward writing on the back of the first sheet.
8. Cut the backward message out, and glue it to the card.

VALENTINE WITHOUT A HEART

MATERIALS: paper, writing tools, scissors, lace, paste

DIRECTIONS:
1. Cut out a two-sided card.
2. Draw a part of the body other than the heart. Examples include a hand, a foot, an ear, or a nose.
3. Cut the part out, and glue it to the card.
4. Add a lace border.
5. Write a silly poem that explains why that body part should be on the valentine—instead of a heart.

My Special Valentine:

To me you smell pretty,
Just like a rose.
So instead of a heart
This card has a nose!

RESOURCES

Card Making Tips

1. For cards that have the look and feel of those bought in a store, use poster board, which can be bought in an art supply shop.

2. To make a four-sided card, first cut out a piece of scratch paper the size each page will be. Use that sheet as a guide to measure the card on the poster board. Then cut out the poster board and carefully fold it, using a ruler to make a clean edge.

3. When writing a poem or a message for a card, first write the words on scratch paper. Feel free to cross out, add, or move words around until the meaning is just right. Then copy the words neatly onto the card.

Poster board

Scratch paper, cut to page size.

Use a ruler to help fold the card evenly.

Write all words on scratch paper first, then copy them onto the card.

Dear Granpa,
I hope you'll come soon and visit us before June.

4. When making a headline for a card, first print the letters lightly in pencil to get the spacing right. Then go over the letters in ink or crayon. If necessary, gently erase the pencil marks.

5. Lettering can also be done by clipping words from newspapers and magazines. Another way to create fancy letters is to use a computer.

6. To make photocopies of a two-sided card, prepare a master copy. For best results, the art should consist of simple, black lines, and the lettering should be dark and crisp. (Color copies can be made, but they cost a lot more.) After copying the first side, put the paper back into the machine and copy side two. Test one copy to make sure the second side prints the right way. Later, color can be added by hand.

Calendar of Special Events

Note: The name of a person designates his or her birthday.

January (Hobby Month)
1 Pun Day
4 Trivia Day
6 Carl Sandburg
8 Elvis Presley
15 Martin Luther King, Jr.
16 National Nothing Day
17 Ben Franklin
18 Pooh Day
23 National Handwriting Day
27 Wolfgang Amadeus Mozart
28 Swap-a-brown-bag-lunch Day
31 Jackie Robinson

February (Friendship Month)
1 Freedom Day
2 Groundhog Day
6 Babe Ruth
7 National Inventor's Day
8 Boy Scouts of America
9 Amy Lowell
11 Thomas Edison
12 Abraham Lincoln
14 Ferris Wheel Day
15 Susan B. Anthony
22 George Washington

March (Nutrition Month)
1 Pig Day
3 National Anthem Day
5 Crispus Attucks
9 Amerigo Vespucci
13 Uranus discovered
14 Albert Einstein

15 Ides of March
17 St. Patrick's Day
20 Spring
22 Goof Off Day
25 Global Understanding Day
26 Sandra Day O'Connor

April (Humor Month)
1 April Fool's Day
3 Washington Irving
12 First manned space flight
13 Thomas Jefferson
15 Income tax due/Titanic sinking
22 Earth Day
23 William Shakespeare

May (Mother's Day—second Sunday)
1 Law Day
5 Cinco de Mayo
12 Limerick Day
13 Joe Louis
22 Lindbergh's flight
24 Brooklyn Bridge
26 John Wayne
29 Patrick Henry

June (Father's Day—third Sunday)
5 First balloon flight
9 Donald Duck
14 Flag Day
15 Friend's Day
21 Summer
25 Custer's Last Stand

July (Anti-Boredom Month)
4 Declaration of Independence
6 Beatrix Potter
12 Different Colored Eyes Day
16 First A-bomb exploded
22 Pied Piper Anniversary
26 Esperanto Day

August (Clown Week—first week)
1 Twins' Day
13 Alfred Hitchcock
15 Napoleon Bonaparte
17 David Crockett
19 Aviation Day
26 Women's Equality Day

September (Labor Day—first Monday)
2 Christa McAuliffe
10 Swap Ideas Day
16 Mayflower Day
17 Citizenship Day
21 Gratitude Day
22 Hobbit Day
23 Autumn
26 Johnny Appleseed
27 Good Neighbor Day
30 Ask a "Stupid" Question Day

October
2 Snoopy's first appearance
9 Benjamin Banneker
12 Columbus Day
13 Molly Pitcher
15 Grouch Day
16 Noah Webster
21 Electric lightbulb
31 Halloween

November (Thanksgiving—fourth Thursday)
1 Author's Day
2 Daniel Boone
3 Sandwich
5 Guy Fawkes Day
6 Saxophone
8 X-ray
11 Veterans' Day
19 Gettysburg Address

December (Human Rights Month)
1 Rosa Park's Day
3 Heart transplant
10 Emily Dickinson
15 Bill of Rights
16 Ludwig Beethoven
17 First airplane flight
22 Winter
25 Christmas
31 Make-Up-Your-Mind Day

Art Ideas

Use the following pictures for ideas to illustrate greeting cards. These pictures may be copied by hand or by a photocopy machine.

Drawing Tips

HOW TO DRAW A FACE

HOW TO DRAW A CAT

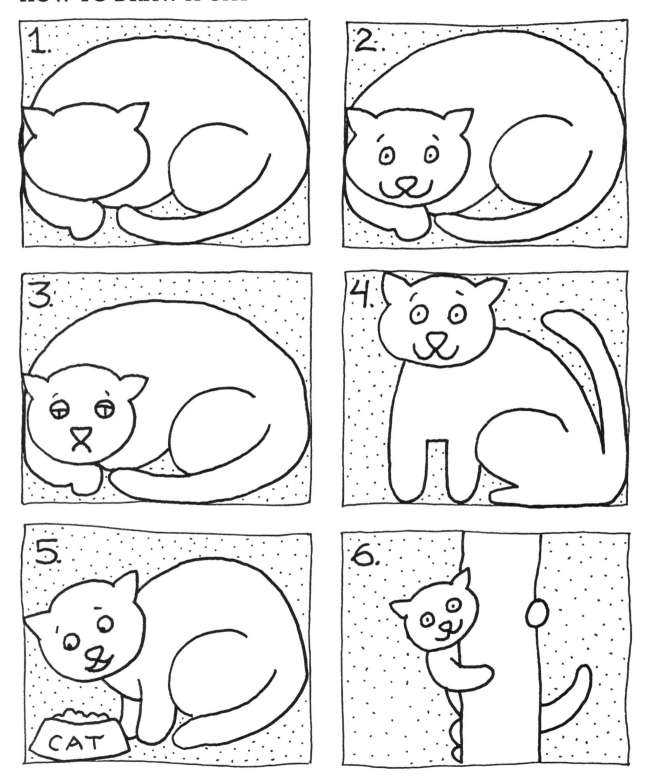

Lettering Ideas

Creative lettering can add eye-appeal to any card.

Yarn attached with tape:

Words cut from newspapers or magazines:

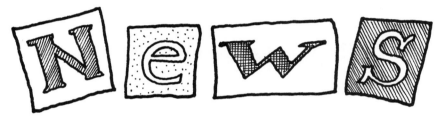

Letters cut from wrapping paper, magazines, or other materials:

Stenciled letters:

Rhyming Dictionary

April/daffodil
August/pie crust/robust/stardust
aunt/can't
baby/maybe
better/letter/wetter
birth/earth/mirth/worth
birthday/earth day/mirth day
brother/mother/another
celebrate/educate/imitate/participate
Chanukah/hurrah hurrah
Christmas/we bless/express/oneness
congratulate/celebrate
cousin/dozen
cute/fruit/hoot/lute/root/toot
dad/glad/had
day/ray/say
December/remember
flower/power/shower
food/dude/rude
Friday/my day/pie day/try day
friend/bend/end/lend/mend/send
fun/one/pun/run/sun/ton
ghost/boast/most/toast
gift/lift/sift
grad/glad/sad
graduation/adulation/celebration
Halloween/in between/don't be mean
happy/sappy/scrappy/snappy
health/wealth
heart/art/dart/part

holiday/jolly day
house/mouse
invitation/celebration
jingle/mingle/single
July/goodbye/mud pie/reply/standby
June/dune/loon/moon/tune
Kris Kringle/jingle jingle
letter/better/wetter
March/arch/parch
May/bay/day/hay/pay/ray/say/way
mom/calm/palm
money/bunny/funny/honey/sunny
mother/brother
New Year/do year
nice/ice/mice
November/remember
older/bolder/colder/shoulder
parent/content/event/present
party/smarty
Saturday/chatter day
school/mule/rule/tool
September/remember
sick/quick/thick/trick
smile/dial/file/I'll/mile/while
thanks/banks/blanks/clanks/pranks
trip/clip/drip/flip/sip/slip/tip
vacation/celebration/graduation
valentine/porcupine/super fine
well/bell/dell/fell/sell
wish/dish/fish

CHILDREN'S FURNITURE YOU CAN MAKE

Complete Plans and Instructions
for Bunks and Bureaus, Chests and Chairs,
Cradles and Computer Tables

Paul Gerhards

STACKPOLE
BOOKS

Published by
STACKPOLE BOOKS
5067 Ritter Road
Mechanicsburg, PA 17055

Printed in the United States of America

Photos and illustrations by Paul Gerhards
Cover design by Caroline Miller

First Edition

10 9 8 7 6 5 4 3 2 1

**Library of Congress Cataloging-in-
Publication Data**

Gerhards, Paul.
    Children's furniture you can make /
Paul Gerhards.
        p.   cm.
    ISBN 0-8117-2534-0
    1. Children's furniture—Amateurs'
manuals. I. Title.
TT197.5.C5G47   1993
684.1′04—dc20   92-42008
                              CIP

*For Daniel, Philip, Patrick,
AJ, David, and Kathryn*

    Where applicable, furniture described in this
book complies with standards set by the U.S.
Consumer Products Safety Commission.

▪ Contents ▪

▪ Tools, Lumber, and Hardware ▪

TOOLS OF THE TRADE

One of the most intimidating things about many crafts and hobbies is the amount of equipment available for pursuing them. Woodworking is no exception. A novice flipping through any woodworking magazine or catalog cannot help being overwhelmed by the variety (and cost!) of the myriad tools and devices available to help perform any job better and faster.

Surprisingly enough, very few of these are absolutely necessary. Craftsmen made furniture for centuries without so much as a spark of electricity.

Of course, many an old-time master craftsman had perhaps dozens of apprentices who did nothing but plane boards to thickness or chop mortises day in and day out, with little more to show for their labor than blisters on their hands and a place to sleep among the wood shavings.

Now, electric power tools can do in an hour what it took a guildhall full of apprentices to do in a month. This means that any woodworker with moderate skills and a minimum of modern equipment can accomplish what the masters created.

So what's a minimum of equipment?

That's a hard question to answer. Any woodworker who's been at it for a while knows that the best way to furnish a shop is not all at once, but over time, buying each tool as it's needed.

A table saw for ripping boards and a radial-arm saw for cutting them to length are a must for any shop. These tools can also perform a variety of other useful functions.

A router and a good collection of bits are indispensable. (Specific bits needed are mentioned at the beginning of each project.) Many routing jobs are performed by guiding the router over the piece. If you can mount the router on a table, however, the functionality of the tool is dramatically increased. What's more, if you mount an incremental fence (such as the Incra Jig) to the table, your accuracy will be increased.

All drawers described in this book are joined with router-cut dovetail joints. If you prefer this method, you will need a dovetail jig for freehand routing or an incremental fence for table-mounted routing.

A relatively new tool on the market is the plate joiner. It's designed to cut matching slots in opposing pieces. The slots then receive compressed hardwood "biscuits" that, when glued in place, expand in the slots to form a strong joint. Several of the projects make use of plate joinery, but you can substitute alternate methods.

A thickness planer, jointer, and drill press are also useful.

Drills and sanders are standard shop equipment, as are measuring devices, chisels, files, clamps, planes, and dozens of other hand tools.

LUMBER

The furniture shown in the photographs in this book is made of either solid pine or oak. The pieces can be made of other kinds of wood, however.

Pine, a softwood, has its drawbacks. Its chief problem is its softness. It's relatively strong and well suited for furniture, but it mars easily during and after construction.

When you use solid wood (as opposed to plywood or other manufactured wood product), measures should be taken to compensate for natural expansion and contraction caused by changes in humidity.

Plywood and MDF

Plywood and its cousin, medium density fiberboard (MDF), have a couple of advantages over solid wood. First, they are stable; they won't expand or contract, and therefore ordinary precautions used in solid-wood construction are unnecessary. Second, because plywood and MDF come in 4' x 8' sheets, you have 32 square feet of uninterrupted surface to work with.

MDF comes plain or with a hardwood veneer on both sides. Used plain, it's suitable for unexposed areas and as a substrate for plastic laminate. Covered with a hardwood veneer it can be substituted for plywood. MDF is, however, considerably heavier than plywood.

The drawback to plywood and MDF is that in most situations the edges must be treated in some way to conceal the core.

Two kinds of plywood are used in the projects presented in this book: fir and oak. Quarter-inch A/C fir is used for backs and drawer bottoms. Quarter-inch A3 oak is used for exposed backs and frame-and-panel sides and doors in several projects. Three-quarter-inch A2 oak is used for shelves and sides in Project 16. The designation A/C (on fir plywood) refers to the grade of the faces, with A being the better side.

Hardwood plywood is also graded by the quality of the faces, with A2 having the highest quality veneer on both sides. A3 has a quality veneer on one side only and is suitable for backs and drawer bottoms, applications where only one side is visible.

HARDWARE

Not all furniture requires hardware, and some pieces use more than others. Hardware used on the projects here can be put in four general categories: screws, nails, and brads; knobs, pulls, and hinges; knock-down (KD) fasteners; and drawer slides.

The standard flathead wood screw, whether slotted or Phillips head, has been replaced in many areas of woodworking by what is commonly called the *drywall screw.* Today, most gypsum board is screwed to studs and joists with a special screw. The thread and "trumpet head" designs are applicable to woodworking, and entire lines of screws have been developed for just that purpose. References to flathead screws are general only.

The projects in this book are assembled with basic joinery techniques. Brads or other small nails are used to secure back panels and for other light-duty tacking jobs; other than that, nails are not used.

Some projects make use of KD fasteners of various descriptions. These fasteners are designed for rapid and repeated assembly and disassembly.

Knobs, pulls, and hinges are a matter of personal preference. Substitute other designs at your discretion.

Several of the projects have drawers. Some of the drawers slide directly on the case's skeletal frame. Others use drawer slides.

For sources of hardware and other materials of interest to woodworkers, see the appendix.

▪ Joinery Notes ▪

Joinery is the art and trade of a joiner, a skilled craftsperson who brings together select pieces of wood to make fine furniture and other products. The basis of the joiner's art is the joints themselves.

A well-made joint serves two purposes: it precisely locates two or more pieces relative to one another, and it locks them together (usually with the help of glue) into a solid unit.

The details of the joint are usually hidden within the case. Casual observers don't notice them. Yet many joints, such as dovetails and through-tenons, are intended to be seen as part of the overall design.

Joints can be divided into two categories: the butt joint, where two pieces abut one another with no overlapping or interlocking surfaces; and the mortise and tenon joint, where one piece fits into the other. There are dozens of variations of these with infinite applications.

A comprehensive discussion of joinery and other furniture-making techniques is not appropriate here, but descriptions of certain joints specific to these projects will be of value.

EDGE JOINT

Several of the projects require large side and top panels of solid wood. These "blanks" are made by gluing two or more boards edge to edge.

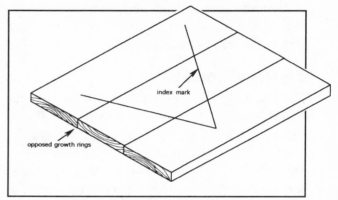

Figure 1. Edge joint

Edges to be joined must be square and smooth, with opposed growth rings (Figure 1). Don't try to join boards that are warped, twisted, or badly cupped. At best, the result will be frustrating.

As a rule, no single board should be wider than eight times its thickness. That means if you're working with one-inch stock, no single board should be wider than eight inches. In practice, the rule isn't absolute and may not always apply, but the theory is sound. The wider the board, the more susceptible it is to cupping. Following the rule, it's best to rip a wide board in two, flip one piece, and then glue them both back together. Moderately cupped boards can be salvaged this way, but more time must be spent making the panel flat.

For most furniture applications reinforcing agents, such as dowels or biscuits, aren't necessary. Although these devices increase the strength of the joint significantly, a properly glued edge joint without reinforcement is itself incredibly strong.

Accurately located dowels or biscuits serve the additional purpose of helping to align the individual boards during clamping. On the other hand, if the reinforcers are inaccurately placed, you will spend even more time working down the surface.

Cut the individual boards so the panel blank will be at least an inch wider and longer than the finished size.

Lay the boards on your workbench face up. Arrange them to your liking. Consider the grain, the way the edges mate, and any defects in the wood. A board with serious defects, of course, should not be used, but minor defects close to an edge can be placed facing out and later ripped away during final sizing.

Once the boards are arranged, mark the panel with a large V. This index will serve to keep mated boards in the right order.

Although the edges must be smooth, do not use any abrasives on them. Abrasives raise tiny fibers, which make for a weaker joint. The best edges are made with a sharp jointer blade, whether hand-held or motor-driven. Either method cuts the fibers cleanly, forming the perfect surface for gluing.

When you're satisfied with the fit, apply an even layer of glue to one or both of the edges. Align the boards using your index marks, and apply clamps. A tiny bead of glue should form along the length of the joint. If it doesn't, you either didn't apply enough glue or the boards weren't mated properly.

DADO AND RABBET CUTS

Some joints are referred to by the joint they make. For example, the edge joint is formed when two square-cut pieces are joined edge

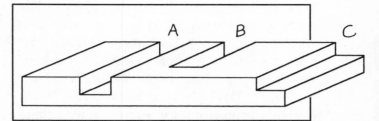

Figure 2. Dado and rabbet cuts. A, through-dado; B, stopped or blind dado; C, rabbet.

to edge. Other joints, such as dadoes and rabbets, are named not for the joint they form, but for the cut that makes them.

A dado is a square channel cut into the field of the board (Figure 2A, B). A rabbet is a cut along the edge of a board (Figure 2C).

It's sometimes undesirable for the dado to go the full width of the board, thereby exposing the joint at its edge. Figure 2B shows a stopped dado. Rabbets can also be stopped.

Obviously something fits into a dado or rabbet cut. A dado might receive a shelf, a frame, or a piece that is itself rabbeted. A rabbeted piece might receive a plywood panel, a shelf, or a frame.

MORTISE AND TENON JOINTS

The mortise and tenon joint (Figure 3) is

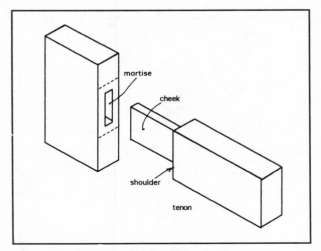

Figure 3. Mortise and tenon joint

used to join relatively narrow pieces. The mortise is the opening into which the tenon fits. A blind tenon fits into a mortise that bottoms out somewhere within the body of the stock. A blind tenon should be about $1/16''$ shy of the bottom of the mortise. Without this repository for excess glue, simple hydraulics can prevent the joint from closing or can shove a closed joint apart. Generally, the tenon is one-third the thickness of the board. If the tenon goes all the way through the stock, it's called a through-tenon.

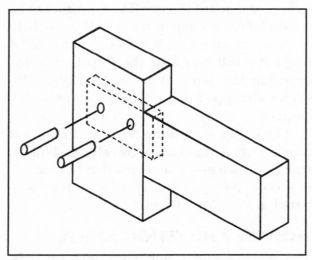

Figure 4. Pinned tenon

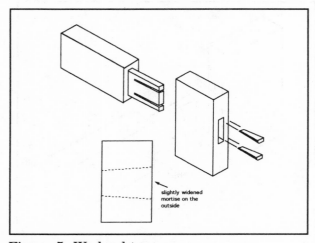

slightly widened mortise on the outside

Figure 5. Wedged tenon

Mortise and tenon joints can be further strengthened with pins (Figure 4) and wedges (Figure 5). For a wedged tenon, the mortise must be widened slightly to accommodate the splay in the tenon caused by the wedge. Cut the tenon slightly longer than necessary, then sand it and the driven wedge flush with the mortised piece.

Three variations of the mortise and tenon joint used extensively in the projects in this book are the stub tenon, the dovetailed tenon, and the sliding dovetail.

Stub Tenon

The stub tenon (Figure 6) is formed by cutting a $1/4'' \times 1/4''$ rabbet on both faces of the first board and a dado of the same size in the second. Such a joint is useful for skeletal framework or frame-and-panel construction of doors and side panels.

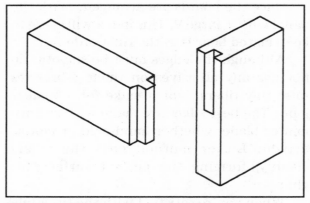

Figure 6. Stub tenon and mortise

Dovetailed Tenon

Most often associated with drawer and box construction, the dovetail joint is also useful in case construction. Notice in Figure 7 how the bearer rail is dovetailed into the case side. The tail is easily cut with two passes on a table-mounted router or by hand with a dovetail saw. Carefully trace the outline of the tail on the case side, and then chop out the mortise with a chisel.

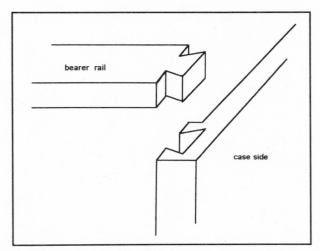

Figure 7. Dovetailed tenon

Sliding Dovetail

The dovetailed tenon works nicely when the rail is at the top of the case. Figure 8 shows how to use a sliding dovetailed tenon to join subsequent front rails to the case. Notice how the side panel is dadoed to receive the frame ends. The dado is stopped from the front a distance equal to the width of the front rail, then extended with a dovetailed slot stopped about ¼″ from the front. It's important to center the slot exactly with the

dado. For obvious reasons the slot cannot be deeper than the dado.

Cutting the tenon for a sliding dovetail joint requires patience. Make trial cuts using scrap stock of the same thickness.

Use a table-mounted router with the dovetail bit set at exactly the same depth as the slot in the side panel. Adjust the fence so the bit takes a small amount off each face of the test piece, until you achieve the desired

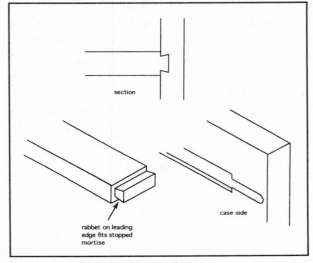

Figure 8. Sliding dovetail

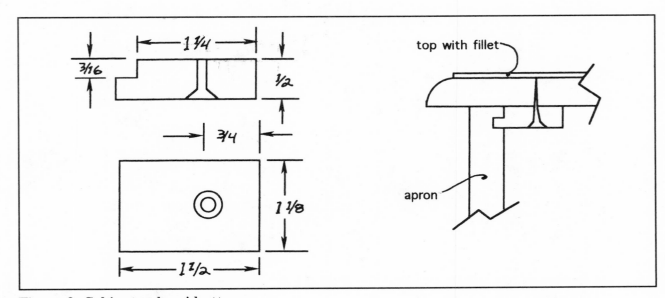

Figure 9. Cabinetmakers' button

width. The best fit is when you can slide the tenon into place under modest pressure.

Cut a rabbet on the leading edge of the tenon to allow for the stopped slot.

▪ **Hint:** If you inadvertently cut a dovetailed tenon too narrow, glue a thin strip of paper to each side.

CABINETMAKERS' BUTTONS

Mounting a tabletop to a frame presents a challenge when the top is glued up from solid stock. The top has to be able to move freely as it expands and contracts. A top solidly secured along each edge will likely split as it contracts.

Solve the problem with cabinetmakers' buttons (Figure 9). Rout a ¼″ x ¼″ groove near the top edge of the table's aprons. The button's rabbeted end fits into the groove, and the button itself is screwed to the top. The top will fit snugly, yet will be able to move as needed.

Commercially available clips made of steel work equally well.

▪ Finishing Notes ▪

A good finish serves several purposes. It seals the wood, thereby lessening the effects of changes in humidity, it protects the wood against damage from day-to-day use, and it enhances the wood's natural beauty.

Finishing is as much a craft as woodworking. Achieving professional results in finishing takes practice. Without proper preparation and without the use of the best tools and materials available, the results will be less acceptable.

Some professionals and experienced woodworker–finishers stick to their own formulas and methods. Others tend to experiment to achieve a specific result. Fortunately, many products on the market today have been developed for ease of application by the do-it-yourselfer.

Several manufacturers offer "systems" of compatible products. It's a good idea to stick with a single brand; don't mix one brand of stain with another brand of top coat. If you are inexperienced with finishing materials, look into one of these systems.

THE IMPORTANCE OF THOROUGH SANDING

Some woodworkers, I've heard, enjoy sanding furniture and get soothing satisfaction from it. I find it one of the most tedious of chores. It doesn't take long, however, to learn that, like it or not, it is a waste of time to put a lot of effort into building a piece and not put sufficient effort into preparing it for finishing.

The purpose of sanding is to make the wood's surface as smooth as possible. This is done in stages, beginning with a coarse sandpaper and progressing to finer and finer grits. Grit refers to the number of abrasive particles per square inch of paper. The lower the number, the coarser the paper; therefore, 80-grit is coarser than 100-grit.

What grit to begin with and how many stages to go through depend on the wood and its condition. In most cases 100-grit is a good choice to start with, but keep in mind that if you start with too coarse a paper, you'll be doing a lot of extra work. The same is true if you start with too fine a grit. More than once I've had to drop down to 100-grit after spending fifteen or twenty minutes not getting anywhere with 150.

A good schedule to follow is 100, 150, 180, 220.

Of course, always sand with the grain, unless you are using an orbital or random-orbital sander. Avoid using power sanders on square corners and edges, especially on softer woods.

The coarser grits—80 and below—are useful for removing a lot of material quickly, especially when used on a power sander.

Sanding belts are readily available in three grits: coarse (50), medium (80), fine (100). Belt-sanders are ideal for removing lots of stock quickly, particularly for smoothing large edge-glued blanks with uneven joints. Again, use the minimum grit necessary to achieve the desired results.

SOLVENTS

Conventional finishing materials have as their vehicle solvents and other ingredients that release volatile organic compounds (VOCs) into the air as they dry. These VOCs have been found to be harmful to the atmosphere. Manufacturers have responded by developing water-soluble finishing products that are ''environmentally safe.'' Many of these products rival the standards.

Environmental concerns aside, water-soluble materials offer other benefits. They are nonflammable and release no explosive fumes. There is no need for flammable solvents for thinning and cleanup, as thinning is usually unnecessary and cleanup is with soap and water. In addition, these products are fast drying, so projects are completed sooner.

Any finish needs to be sanded between coats. Many finishers use 0000 steel wool for this purpose. Steel wool is *not* suitable for use with water-soluble finishes: tiny particles of steel left in the pores will rust. Wet-or-dry paper (400 or 600) is best to use between coats of water-soluble finishes.

▪ Project 1 ▪
CRADLE

In the modern world, the cradle has been replaced by the crib. A well-made crib can be used from the time the newborn is brought home from the hospital until the child is ready for a standard bed. But a cradle offers something a crib cannot: intimacy. Its small size will keep a baby snug and will allow for easy placement near the mother's bed. What's more, when a crib is outgrown, it becomes garage sale fodder. A cradle, though, will give a lifetime of service and may become an heirloom.

Project 1 Material List

Item	Description	Quantity	Thickness	Width	Length	Comments
A	Side	2	3/4″	16″	33″	approximate
B	Headboard	1	3/4″	18″	15¼″	approximate
C	Footboard	1	3/4″	14″	14½″	approximate
D	Bottom	1	½″	12¼″	28¾″	approximate
E	Rocker	2	1½″	4″	22″	
	Flathead screws	22	1½″ x 8″			
	Screw plugs	18	3/8″		diameter	

CONSIDERATIONS

Materials

What wood you use to build the cradle depends on personal taste. The one pictured is made of solid pine, with a ½″ plywood bottom. You will need approximately twenty board feet of lumber.

Special Tools and Cuts

The cradle has just seven pieces. Because of the angles of the sides and ends, special care must be taken during cutting. All the pieces except the bottom have curved cuts, so a band saw or saber saw will be useful. Make the optional pierced cuts in the headboard and footboard with a saber saw.

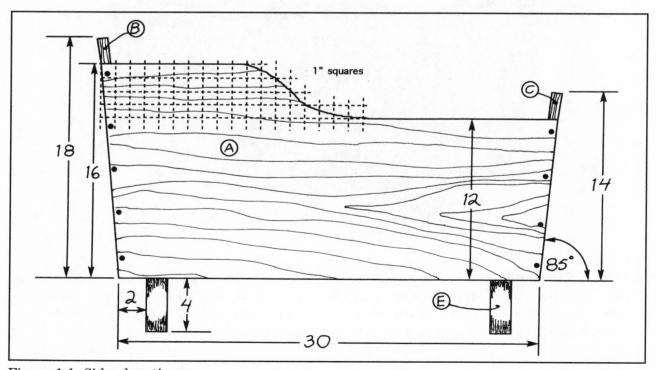

Figure 1.1. Side elevation

PREPARATIONS

Begin the cradle by selecting the boards to glue up into the individual pieces. Notice that the grain runs horizontally in each piece. When assembled this way, the pieces will expand and contract together, reducing the chances of splitting.

Glue up the sides and ends into blanks about 2″ wider and longer than shown in the material list. When the pieces are dry, work them smooth on both sides. Mark the inside and top of each one.

If you can't find stock of suitable size for the rockers, laminate two pieces of ¾″ stock.

CUTTING THE PIECES

Start with the headboard, Part B, and the footboard, Part C. The bottom edge of each piece has a 5° bevel, with the long point on the *inside* (see inset, Figure 1.4).

After you cut the bevel, lay out the side cuts for each end piece. Draw a vertical centerline on the inside of the blank. Measure 6″ each way from the centerline along the

bottom edge. Now draw the 85° lines to establish the side cuts (which are square with the face). Draw the lines as far as they will go. Don't worry about the curved top or the heart cutouts yet. What's important here is that both end pieces are the same width from the bottom up.

Turn your attention to the sides, Parts A. Cut a 5° bevel along the bottom of each edge, again with the long point on the inside. Then lay out and cut the 85° lines.

Lay out the top edge according to the pattern in Figure 1.1. Cutting the top edge square is easiest. A bevel cut, which will

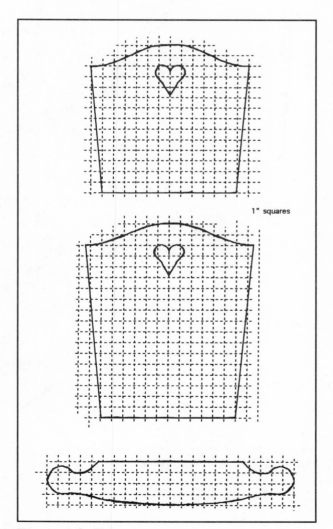

Figure 1.3. Patterns

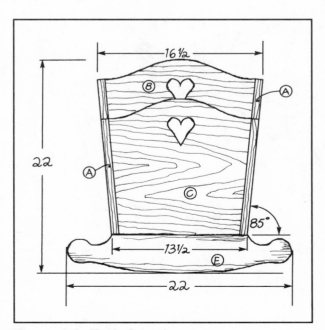

Figure 1.2. End elevation

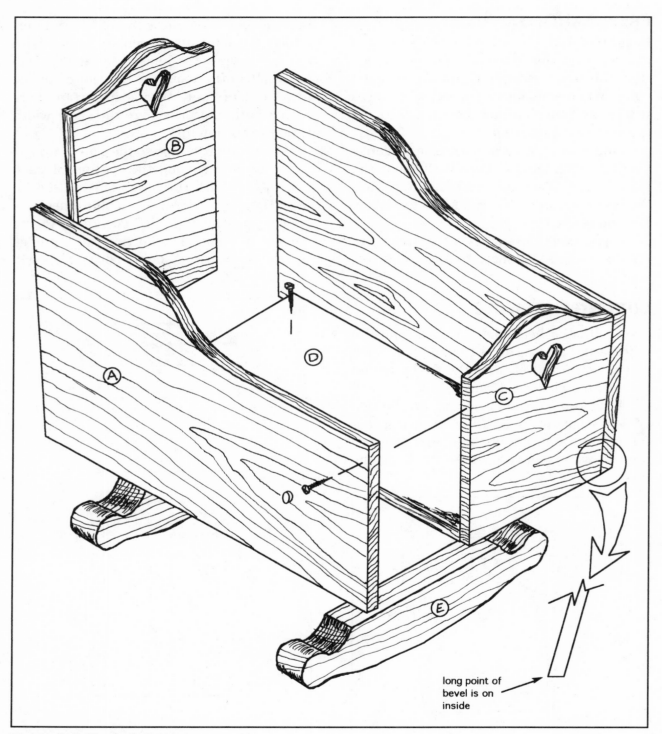

long point of
bevel is on
inside

Figure 1.4. Exploded view

make the top edge parallel with the bottom, will require some fussing through the curved portion of the cut. Smooth out the top edge of each side.

Now lay out the curves on the headboard and footboard as in Figure 1.3. Make the cuts square. Smooth the edges, leaving a little extra wood, ⅛″ or so, toward the sides. This will allow you to work a smooth transition from the ends to the sides after you've assembled the pieces.

Next cut out the heart in each end piece.

Cut the rockers as shown in Figure 1.3. You will cut the bottom later.

ASSEMBLY

Join the sides to the ends with 1½″ x 8 flathead screws. Use five on each side at the head and four on each side at the foot. Lay out the screw placement first, then drill ⅜″ diameter counterbores to receive the screw plugs.

For greater strength, apply a thin layer of glue to the end grain of the headboard and footboard and let it dry.

Start the assembly with the headboard. Apply glue to one edge and bring it into place against its corresponding side. You might need a helper to hold the pieces together while you drill a pilot hole through the lowermost counterbore in the side and into the end grain of the headboard. Secure this point with a screw. Do the same at the top. Repeat the procedure at the remaining corners.

▪ **Note:** If you have a bit that drills a pilot hole and a counterbore at the same time, so much the better.

Turn the frame upside down and check for square by comparing diagonal measurements across the bottom. If they are the same, the unit is square. You may need to push the unit into square. Then drill the rest of the pilot holes and drive the screws home.

Plug the holes with ⅜″ diameter dowel stock.

To fit the bottom, it's necessary to bevel the piece all the way around. A moment of study will reveal that if the bottom is cut to any but the optimal dimensions, it will settle into a position other than flush with the bottom edge of the frame—either too high or too low.

Obtaining the optimal dimensions could be a matter of trial and error, so begin with a piece you know will be a little too large. There is no reason, however, not to leave the bottom a little high. In that case, it will be necessary to use spacers between the bottom and the rockers.

Brush a little glue around the inside of the frame (not the edges of the bottom) and set the bottom into place.

Sand the assembly and the rockers thoroughly.

Glue and tack spacers between the rockers and the bottom if necessary. Secure each rocker with two 1½″ x 8 countersunk flathead screws (longer if necessary).

▪ Project 2 ▪

CHANGING TABLE

One of the most well-used pieces of furniture in a baby's room is the changing table. It's a convenient place to lay the child while you change its diapers and dress it. Also, the changing table helps organize clothing, diapers, and other sundry items a baby needs.

CONSIDERATIONS

Materials

Pine is a good choice for the changing table, although oak or most other furniture-grade wood will work as well. The drawer fronts are made of ³/₄″ stock, and the sides and backs are of ¹/₂″ stock. The case back and the drawer bottoms are ¹/₄″ A/C fir plywood. Make the tray bottom out of ³/₄″ solid stock or plywood. You will need about fifty board feet of lumber, excluding the plywood.

The only hardware necessary for this project are the brads or small nails you will use to hold on the back, the 1¹/₄″ x 8 flathead wood screws for securing the tray to the case, and the knobs for the drawers.

Special Tools and Cuts

You will need these router bits:
  ¹/₄″ straight
  ¹/₄″ round-over
  ¹/₂″ dovetail
  ³/₈″ rabbet with pilot
  ³/₄″ straight

The case frames are assembled with stub tenon joints and let into the case with combination dado–sliding dovetail joints.

The top frame rail, Part B, is dovetailed into the sides.

The toe kick, Part H, has ¹/₄″ x ¹/₂″ rabbet cuts on each end, which form a ¹/₄″ x ¹/₄″ tongue.

The tray has box joints at the front and a simple tongue-and-groove joint in the back (Figure 2.5). The ³/₄″ bottom is rabbeted to fit into a ¹/₄″ x ¹/₄″ groove routed in the sides.

Project 2 Material List

Item	Description	Quantity	Thickness	Width	Length	Comments
A	Side	2	3/4″	18″	33 1/4″	
B	Frame rail	1	3/4″	1 1/4″	35 1/2″	dovetail ends
C	Frame rail	4	3/4″	1 1/4″	35″	sliding dovetail
D	Frame rail	5	3/4″	1 1/4″	35″	
E	Frame end	10	3/4″	1 1/4″	15 3/4″	stub tenon ends
F	Runner/kicker	2	3/4″	4 1/2″	15 3/4″	stub tenon ends
G	Drawer guide	1	3/4″	2 1/2″	12″	
H	Toe kick	1	3/4″	4″	35″	rabbet ends
I	Stile	1	3/4″	2 1/2″	4 1/2″	plate-joined
J	Back	1	1/4″	35 1/4″	29 1/4″	A/C plywood
K	Tray side	2	3/4″	6 3/4″	18 3/4″	
L	Tray back	1	3/4″	6 3/4″	37″	
M	Tray front	1	3/4″	4 3/4″	38″	
N	Tray bottom	1	3/4″	18″	37″	
O	Drawer front	2	3/4″	4 5/8″	16 1/2″	
P	Drawer back	2	1/2″	4 1/4″	15 3/4″	
Q	Drawer side	4	1/2″	4 1/2″	15 3/4″	
R	Drawer bottom	2	1/4″	15 1/4″	15 3/4″	
S	Drawer front	3	3/4″	7 1/8″	35″	
T	Drawer back	3	1/2″	6 3/4″	34 1/4″	
U	Drawer side	6	1/2″	6 3/4″	15 3/4″	
V	Drawer bottom	3	1/4″	15 3/4″	33 3/4″	
	Knobs	8	1 1/4″		diameter	
	Flathead screws		1 1/4″ x 8″		as needed	
	Plate-joinery biscuits	2	#10			

CONSTRUCTING THE CASE

Glue Up Tray Bottom and Side Panels

Select the stock for the tray bottom and case sides and glue up the blanks. Cut the boards so each blank is at least an inch wider and longer than the finished size. Set the tray bottom aside.

  • **Note:** You can use 3/4″ plywood for the tray bottom.

Prepare Sides

When the side panels are dry, scrape away

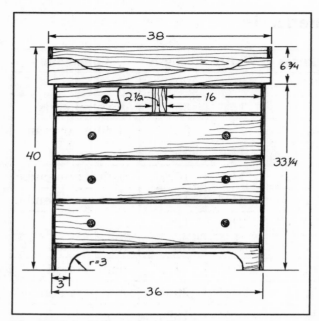

Figure 2.1. Front elevation

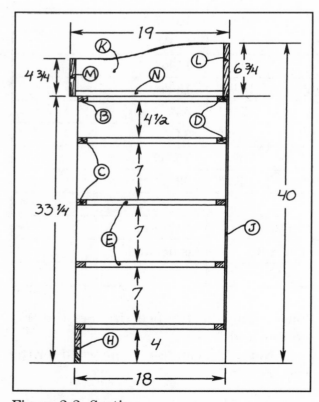

Figure 2.2. Section

any squeezed-out glue and work the panels flat. Cut the sides 18″ wide and 33¼″ long.

Determine which will be the right and left sides. Then determine which edges will be the top and front of each piece. Mark them accordingly on the inside face of each panel.

Cut a ³⁄₈″ x ¼″ rabbet along the inside back edge of the sides to receive the case back, Part J.

Next lay out the dadoes and rabbets for the frames. They are ³⁄₄″ wide and ¼″ deep. Stop the cuts 1¼″ from the front edge of the panel.

Take great care when you lay out and cut the dadoes. Both sides must match exactly. Otherwise, everything will be out of kilter, and the drawers will not fit right.

The frame rails, Parts C, hold the sides together at the front by means of a sliding dovetail. The mortise portion of the joint is ¼″ deep and must be in line with the center of the stopped dado. It is itself stopped about ¼″ from the front edge of the panel.

Cut Dadoes

To cut the dadoes and rabbets for the frames, fit a ³⁄₄″ straight bit into your router and set it to a depth of ¼″. Clamp a straight-edge to the panel as a guide. Stop the cut 1¼″ from the front edge of the panel.

Before removing the guide after each cut, mark its position on the panel for later use when cutting the dovetail mortises.

▪ **Hint:** Two routers, one with a straight bit and the other with a dovetail bit, will speed this process. Be sure the bases are the same so both bits travel along the same centerline.

Once all the dadoes—and the rabbets along the top edges—are cut, chisel out the corners left by the bit.

Cut the ¼″ x ¼″ dado in each side panel for the toe kick, Part H (Figure 2.3).

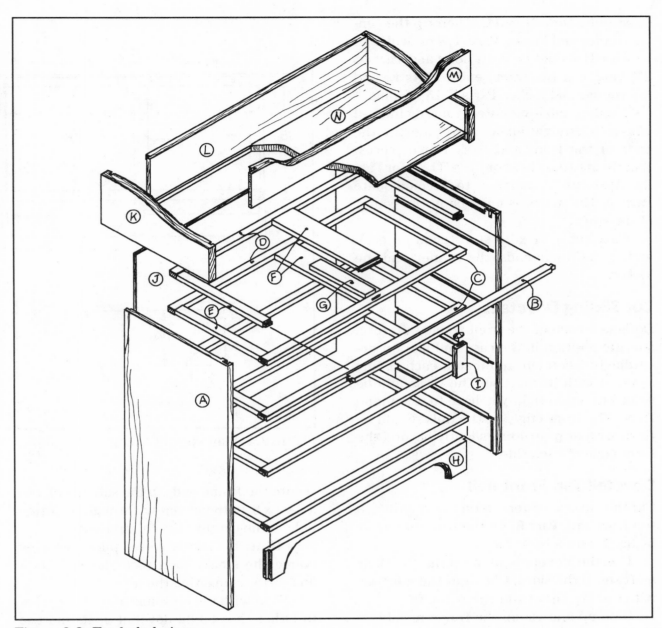

Figure 2.3. Exploded view

Cut Sliding Dovetail Mortises

Put a ½″ dovetail bit into the router and set it to the same depth as the dadoes. Clamp the guide to the marks you set previously. This will orient the dovetail bit in the center of the dado.

Stop the mortises within ¼″ of the front edge of the panel. There is no need to square the inside corners.

You will chop out the dovetailed mortises for the top frame rail, Part B, later.

Cut and Build Frames

Rip enough 1¼″ stock for the frame rails and ends. Choose the best pieces for the front rails, Parts B and C. Then rip the center runner and kicker, Parts F, 4½" wide.

Part B should be 35½" long and Parts C 35" long. Cut the frame ends, Parts E, and the runner and kicker, Parts F, 15¾" long.

Using a table-mounted router chucked with a ¼" straight bit set at ¼", mortise the ends of the front and back frame pieces. Run the mortises in about 1⅜" (1⅝" for Part B). Also cut 5" mortises to accommodate Parts F. The mortises must be in the center of the stock.

Next cut a ¼" x ¼" stub tenon on each end of the frame ends, the runner, and the kicker.

Cut Sliding Dovetails

Designate each of the front frame rails for a specific position in the case and mark it accordingly. Then cut and match each sliding dovetail with its mortise. The fit should be snug, but not so tight you have to use undue force. The front edges of the rails should be flush with or protruding slightly beyond the front edge of each side.

Dovetail Top Front Rail

Cut the dovetailed tenons on the ends of the top front rail, Part B, on the router table or by hand with a backsaw.

Use the dovetails as patterns for their mortises in the sides. Chop out the mortises with a sharp chisel and check the fit.

Glue up and clamp the frame members. Make sure the assembled frame is square.

Finally, cut the center stile, Part I. Then cut slots for a pair of #10 biscuits in both ends of the stile and the upper two front frame rails.

Assemble Case

Because the sides are made of solid wood, and are therefore susceptible to changes in humidity, only the dovetailed portions of the frames should be glued into place. To

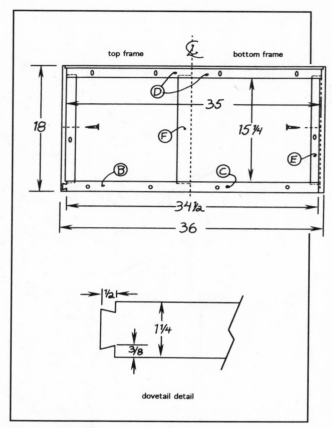

Figure 2.4. Plan view of frames

secure the frame ends to the side panel, use a 1½" x 8 flathead screw through a slotted hole in the center of each frame end.

• **Hint:** To make a slotted pilot hole, first pierce the stock, then rock the drill back and forth, elongating the hole.

Begin with the bottom frame. Apply glue to either the sliding dovetail or its mortise on each side and slip the frame into place. Do not yet drive the screws into the sides.

• **Hint:** Let the rails protrude beyond the side about ¹/₆₄", then sand until flush for a perfect joint.

Bring the subsequent frames into place, saving the top one for last. Install the stile, Part I, before fitting the top frame.

Check the front for square and screw the frame side members to the panels. It may be necessary to draw the sides tight to the

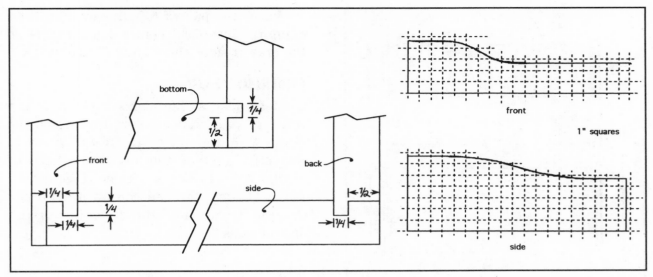

Figure 2.5. Tray patterns and joint details

frame ends with clamps before you drive the screws.

Turn the case over and check the fit of the back. If the back panel is squarely cut, you can use it to square up the back.

Apply a bead of glue to the rails and down the sides. Use ⁵⁄₈″ brads or other small nails to secure the back.

Cut the toe kick, Part H, 4″ wide and 35″ long. Cut a ¹⁄₄″ x ¹⁄₂″ rabbet in each end (leaving a ¹⁄₄″ x ¹⁄₄″ tenon). Then make the cutouts, as shown in Figure 2.1.

Turn the case right side up and install the toe kick. Coat the rabbeted ends of the toe kick with glue and run a bead of glue along its upper edge. Slip it into place and clamp.

Assemble Tray

Rip the tray sides, Parts K, and back, Part L, 6³⁄₄″ wide, and the front, Part M, 4³⁄₄″ wide. Don't cut the scroll work yet.

Cut the pieces to length, then cut the joints as shown in Figure 2.5. Use a table saw or table-mounted router. Also cut the grooves in the front, back, and sides to accommodate the bottom.

Once you've checked the fit of each joint, lay out and cut the curves in the sides and front. Work out the rough edges of the cuts, saving the final smoothing for after you've assembled the tray.

• **Hint:** Before assembling the tray, apply a thin layer of glue to the end grain of the front, back, and sides and let dry. This will seal the grain, preventing the "real" glue from being siphoned away from the joint.

To assemble the tray, glue and join the tray front to one of the sides. Set the bottom into the grooves. Fit the back, and lastly, the other side.

• **Note:** When you install a tray bottom made of solid stock, do not anchor it with glue to both the front and back edges. Doing so will likely cause the panel to split as it dries out. Glue the front edge only. This will keep the panel secure within the tray and still allow it to contract away from the back. Do not let glue from the rear joints anchor to bottom at the corners.

CONSTRUCTING THE DRAWERS

Always consider the effects of humidity on drawers. Drawers made during humid

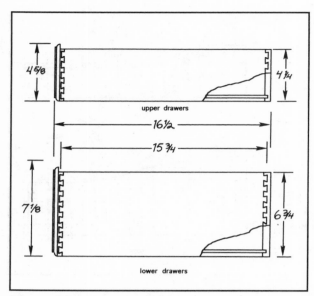

Figure 2.6. Drawer details

Insert the pair of top drawers into their openings. Install the center guide, Part G, so the drawer sides glide easily against it.

FINISHING UP

Sand all pieces thoroughly and apply the finish of your choice before final assembly. If you wish, round over the front corners of the case. To mount the tray, drill a series of slotted holes in the top frame (Figure 2.4). Drive 1¼″ x 8 flathead screws up through the top frame into the tray. Install the drawer pulls.

periods will shrink as they dry out. Those made during dry times will expand in humid weather—sometimes to the extent that they cannot be opened if they were originally made to fit too well. Do not rely entirely on the measurements given in the diagrams and the material list. Rather, use your best judgment based on the wood you've chosen, the region in which you live, and the tolerances you will accept.

The drawers for the changing table have a ⅜″ offset at the top and along the sides. This eliminates the need for stops within the case and allows for greater leeway in fitting.

The drawers shown in Figure 2.6 are dovetailed front and back. This is the strongest construction, but other methods will produce satisfactory results. The length of the sides assumes ¼″ machined dovetails at each end. This will vary according to the bit you use.

Use a ¼″ round-over bit to treat the upper edges of the drawer sides. Use the same bit to round over the edges of the drawer fronts, but leave a ¹⁄₁₆″ fillet (raised edge) for visual effect.

Cut a ¼″ x ¼″ groove for the bottom.

▪ Project 3 ▪
STEP STOOL

All children develop at different rates. At what stage one begins to walk is different for each child. One thing is certain, though: as soon as a kid begins to walk, he begins to explore his world in earnest. Things, however, are always a bit out of reach (intentionally, it often turns out).

An easy-to-carry step stool is one of the first tools a child learns to use on his own. A child with a step stool is a child who begins to expand his own horizons.

CONSIDERATIONS
Materials
The step stool is easily assembled from scrap pieces found around the shop. The one pictured is made of 1 x 12 pine. The pieces are screwed together, and the holes are plugged with ⅜" diameter dowel stock.

Project 3 Material List

Item	Description	Quantity	Thickness	Width	Length	Comments
A	Leg	2	¾"	11"	7³⁄₈"	
B	Stretcher	2	¾"	3½"	10¼"	
C	Top	1	¾"	10"	12"	
	Flathead screws	14	1½" x 8"			
	Screw plugs	14	⅜"		diameter	

Special Tools and Cuts

The legs and stretchers have decorative cuts done on a band saw or with a saber saw. The stretchers are dadoed into the legs. Round over the top with a ¼″ bit in the router.

CUTTING THE PIECES

Cut the legs, Parts A, 7³⁄₈″ long and 11″ wide; the stretchers, Parts B, 3½″ wide and 10¼″ long; and the top, Part C, 12″ long and 10″ wide.

Lay out the decorative curves (Figure

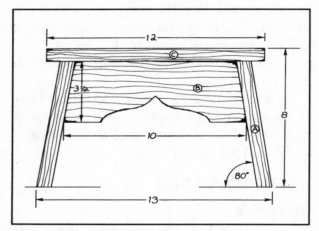

Figure 3.1. Side elevation

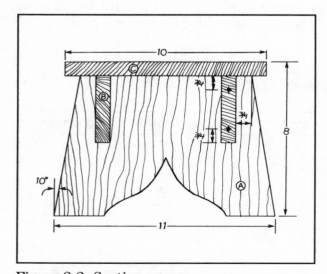

Figure 3.2. Section

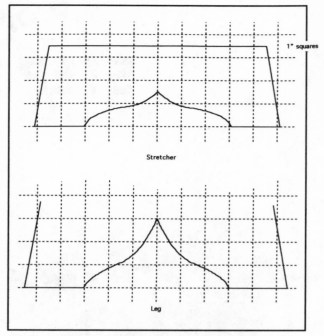

Figure 3.3. Patterns

3.3) and all the other cuts on the legs and stretchers. Put a ¾″ straight bit into your table-mounted router (or dado blade in your radial-arm or table saw) and cut the ⅛″-deep dadoes in the legs.

Next cut the 10° bevel on the top and bottom edges of the legs. Then cut the 10° taper on the legs (Figure 3.2) and cut the angles on the ends of the stretchers.

With a band saw or saber saw cut the curves and sand them smooth.

Lay out and cut the 1″ x 3″ hand-hold in the center of the top. Use a 1″ spade bit or Forstner bit to bore through the ends of the hand-hold. Finish the hand-hold with a saber saw.

When you've smoothed the cuts, mount a ¼″ round-over bit in the router and work the upper and lower edges of the top, including those of the hand-hold.

ASSEMBLY

Lay out the screw holes in the legs. Drill a

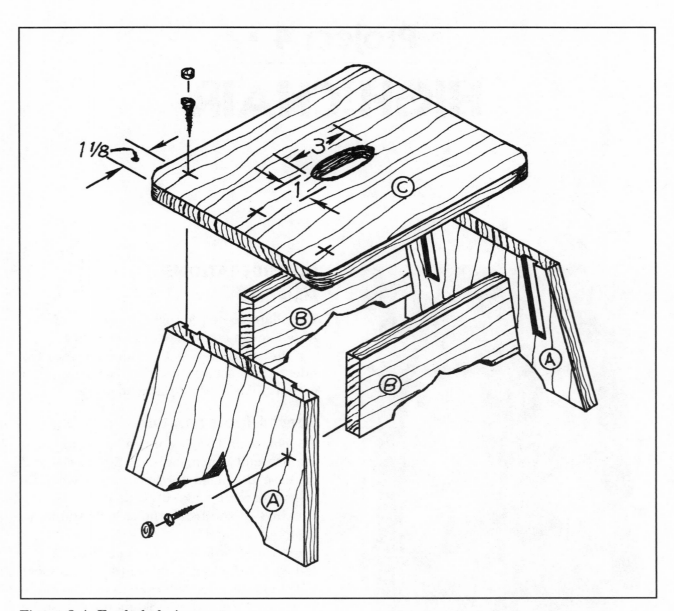

Figure 3.4. Exploded view

³/₈″ counterbore about ³/₁₆″ deep at all locations. Apply glue to the end of a stretcher and into its dado. Hold the stretcher in place and drill pilot holes through the leg and into the stretcher. Then drive the 1¹/₂″ screws. Repeat for the remaining joints.

To plug the holes, apply glue to the end of a length of dowel. Insert the dowel into the counterbore, and use a fine-tooth saw to cut the dowel about ¹/₃₂″ above the surface.

When the glue has set up, but before mounting the top, sand the plugs flush.

Place the top on the base. Locate the screws where they will *not* exit the leg on the inside. Counterbore the screw holes in the top. Apply glue to the top edges of the leg assembly and replace the top. Drill pilot holes and drive home the screws.

Finally, plug the holes and sand smooth.

▪ Project 4 ▪

HIGH CHAIR

The high chair is perfect for the toddler ready to join the family at the dining table. The arms curve down at the front to allow for a close fit at the table. The legs are splayed front to back and side to side for added stability, and the wide steps in front make for easy climbing.

CONSIDERATIONS

Materials

The chair in the photograph is made of oak. About seven board feet are necessary.

The steps and seat are dadoed into the sides, then secured at each bearing point with a single 1½" x 8 flathead screw.

Special Tools and Cuts

The compound angles of the legs compound the difficulty in laying out the pieces and increase the need for accuracy. Overcome this obstacle by making precise, full-scale drawings of the front and side as shown in Figures 4.1 and 4.2.

You also will need a means to cut the dadoes for the steps and seat at the correct angle. Figure 4.6 shows how to make a guide for routing the dadoes. The job can also be done on a radial-arm saw.

All edges are eased with a ¼" round-over bit.

The stretchers and back are joined to the legs with #20 biscuits. This can also be accomplished with dowels or mortise and tenon joints, with an obvious increase in difficulty. The beauty and ease of plate joining, however, become apparent when applied to this project.

Make several wedges out of ¾" pine stock to use as clamp blocks. The wedges are

Project 4 Material List

Item	Description	Quantity	Thickness	Width	Length	Comments
A	Leg	4	3/4"	2 1/2"	30"	all measurements
B	Arm	2	3/4"	3 1/2"	12"	include extra
C	Seat back	1	3/4"	3 1/2"	13"	width and length
D	Rear stretcher	1	3/4"	3 1/2"	15"	
E	Side stretcher	2	3/4"	3 1/2"	12"	
F	Bottom step	1	3/4"	3 1/2"	15 1/2"	
G	Top step	1	3/4"	3 1/2"	14 1/2"	
H	Seat	1	3/4"	15"	13 1/2"	grain runs side to side
	Flathead screws	8	1 1/2" x 8"			
	Screw plugs	8	3/8"			diameter
	Plate-joinery biscuits	12	#20			

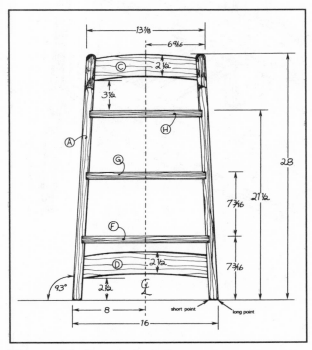

Figure 4.1. Front elevation

necessary to ensure even clamping pressure
across the assemblies when gluing up.

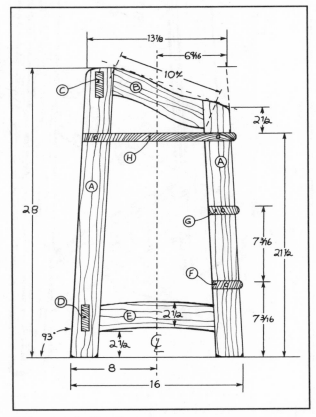

Figure 4.2. Section

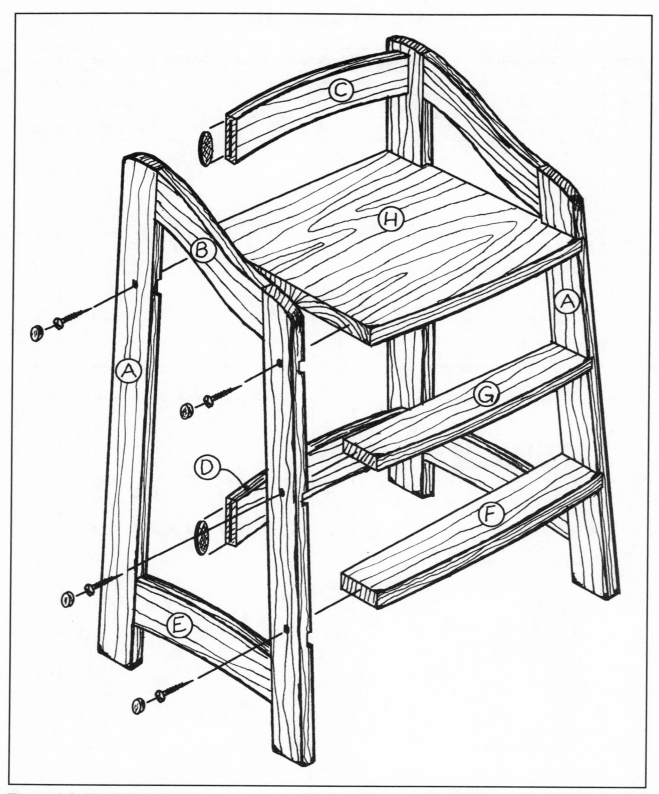

Figure 4.3. Exploded view

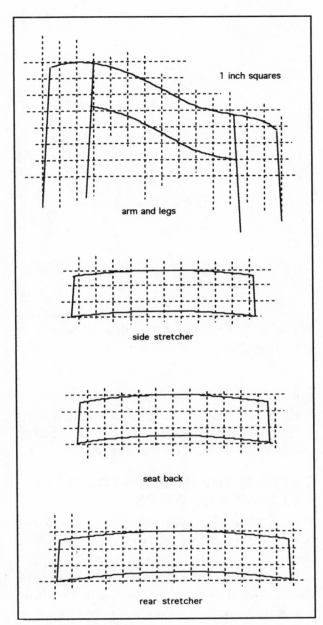

1 inch squares

arm and legs

side stretcher

seat back

rear stretcher

Figure 4.4. Patterns

CUTTING AND ASSEMBLING THE SIDES

Rip the legs, Parts A, 2½″ wide and cut them about 30″ long. Rip the arms, Parts B; seat back, Part C; stretchers, Parts D and E; and steps, Parts G and F, at least 3½″ wide. Cut the arms at least 2″ longer and the other components 1″ longer than indicated in the drawings. Glue up the seat blank, Part H, and set it aside.

Place a pair of legs directly on your full-scale drawing, outside up. Let the ends run wild. Mark the bottom of each leg and the points where the arm and stretcher meet the legs.

Notice that initially both sides are the same and the pieces can be laid out on the same plan. At some point, though, you will have to make a distinction between right and left. Although this might seem obvious and not worth mentioning, the importance becomes apparent when you consider the angles of the feet and of the dadoes into which the steps fit. When you index the feet with the pattern, the short point of the bevel is on the *inside* of the leg assemblies (see Figure 4.1).

Don't cut the feet yet. Instead, keep the extra length for insurance. If something moves out of alignment during assembly, little harm will be done.

Put the legs aside and place one of the arms on the drawing. Mark and cut the upper, or rearmost, angle and check the fit against the leg. Cut the same angle on the other arm. Now cut the angles on the lower, or forward, end of each arm.

• **Hint:** Cut the angles on a piece of scrap stock first to make sure they are correct.

Next, cut and fit the side stretchers.

Now, following the diagrams in Figure 4.4, make patterns for the side stretchers and the arms. Notice the parallel arcs that describe the stretchers are, at their center points, ½″ and 3″ above the bottom edge of the stock. This results in a stretcher 2½″ wide throughout the sweep.

Trace the pattern onto the stock, but don't cut the curves just yet. You'll see why when you cut the slots for the biscuits, which is the next step. Drawing the curves locates the boundaries for the slots, but it's easier to do the slotting first.

Once you've made the slots, cut the curves in the stretchers and the bottom of the arm. Don't cut the curves in the upper edge of the arms and the top ends of the legs. You will do this after assembly to ensure a smooth transition. Smooth out the curves with a belt sander or drum sander.

Apply glue to the biscuits and the ends of the components. Bring the pieces together, checking for proper alignment. Clamp and set the assemblies aside.

When the side assemblies are dry, cut and sand the curves along the top edges of the arms. Make sure all the joints are flush on both sides.

PREPARING THE SEAT BACK AND REAR STRETCHER

The seat back and rear stretcher are fitted and cut in the same fashion as the arms and side stretchers, but there are two important distinctions regarding placement. First, the pieces are set in about ¾″ from the back edge of the legs. Second, rather than following the incline of the legs, they are perpendicular to the horizontal. Both jobs can be accomplished at once with the plate joiner, but there are a couple of things that must be done first.

First, ensure that the cutter in your plate joiner is set to cut a slot in the center of the stretcher and seat-back stock. Then cut the slots. Now *raise* the cutter. The amount you raise it (I cranked mine up as far as it would go) will determine the offset of the seat back and stretcher from the back edge of the legs.

Next make a wedge with a 3° taper. This wedge, when glued temporarily to the back edge of the leg, will orient the plate joiner to 90° from the horizontal (Figure 4.5). The wedge should taper to nothing and be long enough to support the entire length of the plate joiner's base.

Center the wedge on the centerline of

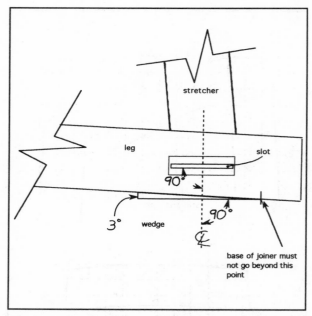

Figure 4.5. Cutting slots for seat back and rear stretcher

the slot and tack the wedge in place with a couple of dabs of hot glue or spray-mount adhesive. The wedge must not slide during the slotting operation. Cut the slots.

CUTTING THE DADOES FOR THE SEAT AND STEPS

The seat and steps are fitted into dadoes cut into the legs. Now is not the time to cut them if you plan to round over the edges with a ¼″ bit (the bit's pilot will drop into the dadoes and damage the legs). But now is the time, while the edges are still square, to lay out the dadoes and cut the legs to length.

Cut the compound angles on the feet on a radial-arm saw or by hand with a backsaw. Make sure you have the blade and arm oriented correctly for each cut. It's too easy to ruin the entire project by cutting one leg backward.

Once the legs are cut and the dadoes laid out (check the orientation), round over the edges of the side assemblies, inside and out.

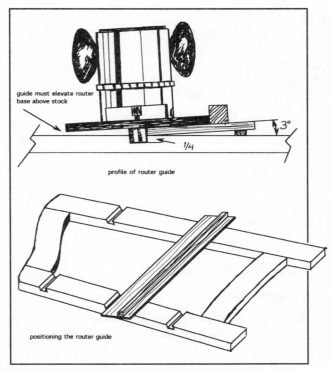

guide must elevate router base above stock

3°

1/4

profile of router guide

positioning the router guide

Figure 4.6. Routing the dadoes

Now cut the dadoes. Use a radial-arm saw fitted with a sharp, clean-cutting dado head or a router with a ¾″ straight bit.

• **Note:** Using a router requires a shop-made guide to orient the base of the router 3° from horizontal (Figure 4.6). Align the edge of the guide with the line marking the lowermost edge of the dado and clamp it down. Set the bit at about ¼″ plus the thickness of the guide where its edge meets the assembly.

FITTING THE SEAT AND STEPS

As with the other components, the seat and steps should be fitted before shaping. Begin by dry assembling the seat back and rear stretcher to the sides, using a clamp across each member.

Measure the distance between the seat dadoes at the rear of the assembly and cut the seat to this length. Bevel the back edge of the seat (and the steps, while you're at

it, but with a reverse bevel) to match the incline of the legs. Slip the seat into place (temporarily remove the clamps if necessary) and make it flush at the back. Clamp the front together at the seat.

Check that the legs are splayed equally at the front and back. Measure for the bottom step. Slip the step into place and clamp. Then fit the top step.

When you're satisfied that everything is aligned, pre-drill and counterbore holes for the 1½″ x 8 flathead screws where indicated.

Next, mark the junctures where the leading edges of the seat and steps meet the legs, then disassemble the components. Lay out and cut arcs similar to those on the stretchers, but only on the leading edges. Then round over the front edges and sand with 150-grit paper before assembling.

FINAL ASSEMBLY

Working quickly, glue up and assemble the horizontal members to one side, then bring the other side into place and clamp. Drive home the screws, and set the assembly aside to dry.

Clean up any stray glue and sand with 220-grit. Then plug the screw holes.

Place the chair on a flat surface and check for wobble. Trim the feet if necessary.

Finish in the method of your choice.

▪ Project 5 ▪
NIGHTSTAND

It's always nice to have a small piece of furniture near the bed on which to put a lamp, a clock, or a book of bedtime stories. The nightstand is just the thing. It has a small drawer at the top and storage cupboard beneath.

CONSIDERATIONS
Materials
Made of solid pine, the nightstand matches most of the other bedroom furniture presented in this book. Build two, and they will go perfectly with the convertible bunk beds in the twin configuration.

The drawer front is flush with the case and made of 3/4" stock. The drawer sides and back are 1/2".

The bottom and the optional middle shelf can be made of solid stock or edged plywood.

The back and drawer bottom are 1/4" plywood.

You will need about twenty board feet of lumber, excluding the plywood.

Special Tools and Cuts
You will need these router bits:
   1/4" straight
   1/4" round-over
   1/2" round-over
   1/2" dovetail
   3/8" rabbet bit with pilot
   3/4" straight
The two frames are assembled with mortise and stub-tenon joints. The frame that supports the drawer is let into the case with a combination dado–sliding dovetail.

Project 5 Material List

Item	Description	Quantity	Thickness	Width	Length	Comments
A	Side	2	3/4"	14"	23 1/4"	
B	Frame rail	1	3/4"	1 1/4"	15 1/2"	dovetail ends
C	Frame rail	1	3/4"	1 1/4"	15"	sliding dovetail ends
D	Frame rail	2	3/4"	1 1/4"	15"	square ends
E	Frame end	4	3/4"	1 1/4"	11 3/4"	stub tenon ends
F	Middle shelf	1	3/4"	12 7/8"	15"	
G	Bottom	1	3/4"	13 3/4"	15"	
H	Toe kick	1	3/4"	3"	15"	rabbet ends
I	Back	1	1/4"	15 1/4"	20 1/4"	plywood
J	Top	1	3/4"	14 1/2"	17"	
K	Door rail	4	3/4"	1 1/2"	7 1/4"	plate join to panel
L	Door panel	2	3/4"	7 1/4"	11 1/4"	
M	Drawer front	1	3/4"	3 5/8"	14 3/8"	
N	Drawer back	1	1/2"	3 5/8"	14 3/8"	
O	Drawer side	2	1/2"	3 5/8"	12 1/4"	
P	Drawer bottom	1	1/4"	12 1/4"	13 7/8"	plywood
	Knobs	4	1 1/4"			diameter or equivalent
	Hinges	2	pr.			brass butt or surface mount
	Flathead screws	6	1 1/4" x 8"			
	Flathead screws	4	1 1/2" x 8"			

The top frame is let into a 1/4" x 3/4" rabbet, with the front rail, Part B, dovetailed into each side.

The toe kick, Part H, has 1/4" x 1/2" rabbet cuts on each end (forming a 1/4" x 1/4" tongue).

The back is let into a 1/4" x 3/8" rabbet.

Use the 1/4" round-over bit to treat the upper edges of the drawer sides and the front corners of the case.

Round over the upper edges of the top with the 1/2" bit, leaving a 1/16" fillet, or cut a decorative edge of your choice.

CONSTRUCTING THE CASE
Glue Up Sides, Top, and Shelves

Select the boards for the sides, top, and shelves and glue up the blanks. Make them

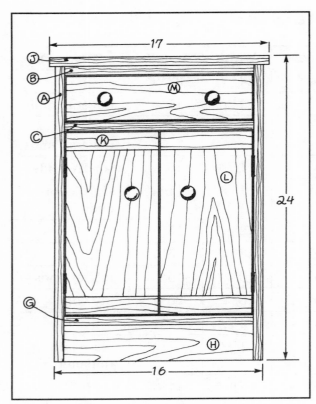

Figure 5.1. Front elevation

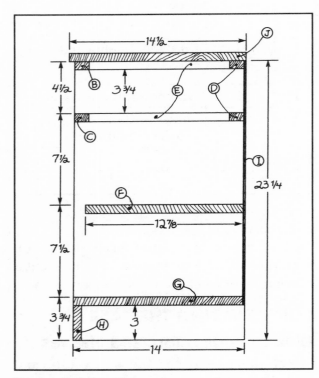

Figure 5.2. Section

an inch or more larger than necessary. When they are dry, work the blanks smooth. Set the top and shelves aside.

Prepare Sides

Cut dadoes. Cut the sides 14″ wide and 23¼″ long. Then cut the ¼″ x ³⁄₈″ rabbets for the back.

Now lay out the dadoes for the frames and shelves. Stop the dadoes and rabbet cuts for the frames 1¼″ from the front edge of the side. Stop the dadoes for the bottom shelf at least ¼″ from the front and the dadoes for the middle shelf ⁷⁄₈″ from the front.

Use a ³⁄₄″ straight bit in the router to cut the dadoes ¼″ deep. Run the router against a guide clamped to the stock. Mark the position of the guide after making the cuts for the drawer-runner frame. You will refer to the marks later. Chisel out the excess left in the corners by the bit.

Cut dovetailed mortises. The front rail of the drawer-runner frame, Part C, slips into a sliding-dovetail mortise.

Put the ½″ dovetail bit into the router and set it to the same depth as the dado. Clamp the guide into the same position as it was when you cut the dado. Cut the dovetailed mortises, stopping them within ¼″ of the front edge.

You will cut the dovetailed mortises for the top front frame rail, Part B, later.

Now cut the ¼″ x ¼″ groove for the toe kick, Part H.

Build Frames

Select the stock for the frames and rip it 1¼″ wide. Cut the top front rail, Part B, 15½″ long and the others, Parts C and D, 15″ long. The four frame ends, Parts E, are 12″ long. Bore a slotted pilot hole horizontally through the center of each frame end.

Cut stub tenons on the frame ends, then mortise the ends of the rails with a ¼″

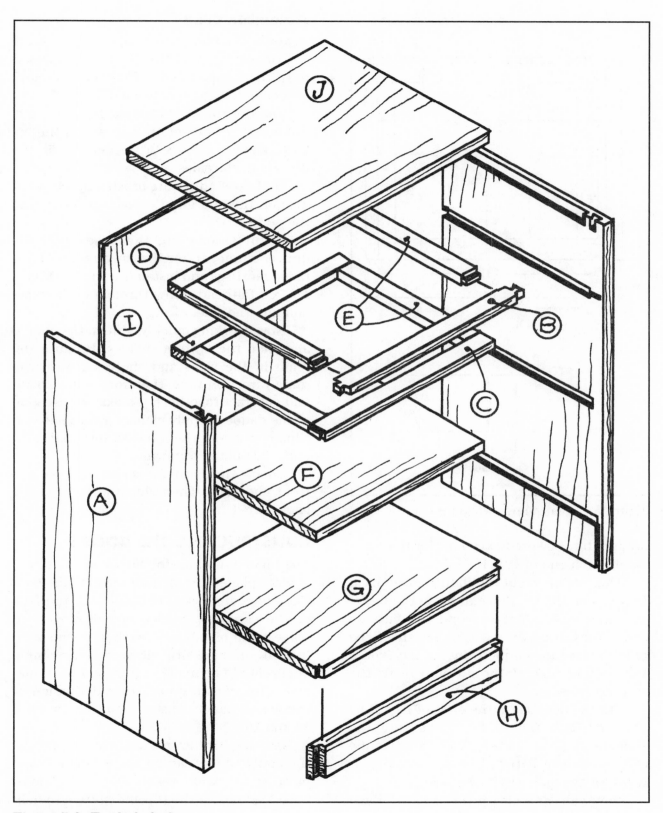

Figure 5.3. Exploded view

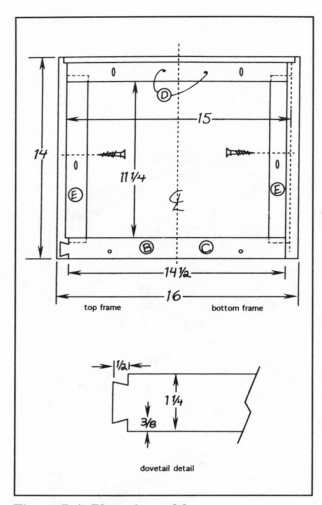

Figure 5.4. Plan view of frames

straight bit. Be sure to account for the extra ¼" on each end of Part B.

Then set up to cut the sliding dovetails in Part C. Use the ½" dovetail bit in the table-mounted router. Make several test cuts on scrap stock to get the right fit. You should be able to just tap the piece into place. Notch the leading edge of the dovetail to fit the stopped mortise.

Cut the dovetail in the ends of Part B by hand or with the router. Make sure the shoulder-to-shoulder length of Part B is the same as that of Part C. Use the tails as patterns for the mortises in the sides.

Now glue and clamp the frames. Make sure they are square.

Assemble Case

Before assembling the case, cut the bottom and middle shelves. Notch the bottom shelf to fit the stopped dado. No other treatment is needed for the middle shelf.

Cut the toe kick 3" wide and 15" long. Cut a ¼" x ½" rabbet on each end of the toe kick (leaving a ¼" x ¼" tenon) to fit the grooves in the sides.

For better adhesion, brush a thin layer of glue on the end grain of each piece to seal the pores.

Begin assembling the case with the drawer-runner frame. Brush glue into dove-tailed mortises and install the frame. Drive a 1¼" x 8 flathead screw through each frame end into the side.

Now, working quickly, glue in the middle and then the bottom shelves. Because the grain in the sides and shelves run in the same direction (and therefore will expand and contract together), it's okay to use glue in the dadoes. Apply clamps where needed. Glue and clamp the toe kick into place. Finally, install the top frame.

Check the case for square across the front and back. Then glue and tack on the back, Part I.

CONSTRUCTING THE DOORS

The nightstand has double doors to accommodate placement on either side of the bed. The doors are mounted flush with the face of the case. You might, however, wish to make a pair of cabinets, each with one door, hinged on opposite sides. Larger single doors should be made of plywood or frame-and-panel construction. For a discussion of frame-and-panel construction, see Projects 14 and 16.

Because of their narrow widths, each of the double doors can be made from a single piece of available stock. Those illustrated have 1½" rails at the top and bottom to help keep the doors flat. Join each rail to its door with a pair of #10 biscuits or a tongue-and-groove joint. If you use a tongue-and-groove joint, be sure to add the extra ½″ in length. Make the doors a little large for custom fitting.

Sand the door faces and cut the panels to give about 1/16″ clearance all around. Mount the hinges and check the fit. Adjust as necessary and remove for finishing.

CONSTRUCTING THE DRAWER

The flush drawer is machine dovetailed front and back. Other methods of construction are, of course, acceptable. The measurement given for the drawer sides assumes ¼″-long dovetails at each end. The actual length will vary according to the bit used.

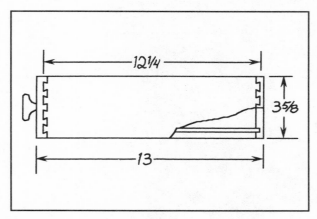

Figure 5.5. Drawer detail

Before assembly, round over the top edges of the sides and sand all pieces on their inner sides. After assembly, sand the joints smooth and check the fit. Use a block plane to make any adjustments.

With the face of the drawer flush with the front of the case, glue and screw a stop on one of the runners.

FINISHING UP

Cut the top to the correct dimensions and rout a decorative edge along the front and each side.

Sand all surfaces thoroughly and apply finish. Mount the doors and put the knobs on the doors and drawer. Drill a series of slotted pilot holes in the top frame. Secure the top with 1¼″ x 8 flathead screws driven through the frame from the bottom.

▪ Project 6 ▪
TOY BOX

As any parent knows, the quantity of toys a child collects grows at least as fast as the child. At the end of a busy day, a roomy toy box is just the place to make a room full of toys disappear in a hurry.

CONSIDERATIONS
Materials

Pine is a good choice for the toy box. You will need about twenty-eight board feet,

Project 6 Material List

Item	Description	Quantity	Thickness	Width	Length	Comments
A	Front/back	2	3/4″	17 1/4″	36″	
B	Side	2	3/4″	17 1/4″	18″	
C	Cleat	2	3/4″	3/4″	34 1/2″	
D	Cleat	2	3/4″	3/4″	15″	
E	Bottom	1	1/2″	16 1/2″	34 1/2″	plywood
F	Lid	1	3/4″	18 1/2″	34″	
G	Lid end	2	3/4″	1 1/2″	18 1/2″	
	Lid support	2				L&R end-mount, meets CPSC
	Bumper	2				
	Piano hinge	1	1 1/2″ x 36″			continuous
	Flathead screws		1 1/4″ x 8″			as needed
	Handle	2				optional
	Plate-joinery biscuits	6	#10			

excluding the 1/2″ plywood bottom. The lid swings on a 36″ continuous brass hinge. The lid is supported by a pair of left- and right-mount spring-loaded supports. These are designed to keep the lid open at any position, as specified by the U.S. Consumer Products Safety Commission. This is to prevent the lid from accidentally dropping on a child's head, neck, or fingers.

Special Tools and Cuts

The finger-joint construction of the toy box elevates the piece from run-of-the-mill to keepsake quality. Although this method is time consuming and challenging, the visual interest of the alternating face and end grain is its own reward.

To make the hand-cut finger joints you will need a fine-tooth dovetail saw, a coping saw, and a 3/4″ chisel. A Japanese-style dove-tail saw, which cuts on the pull stroke, is ideal.

The lid ends, Parts G, are each joined to the lid with three #10 or #20 plate-joinery biscuits.

GLUE UP BLANKS

Begin by gluing up boards into panels for the front, back, sides, and lid. Make sure the panels are as flat and even across their faces as possible.

Rip the front, back, and sides 17 1/4″ wide. Cut the front and back 36 1/8″ long and the sides 18 1/8″ long.

▪ **Note:** The extra 1/8″ allows for the fingers to run 1/16″ long at each corner. Then, after assembly, you can sand them flush with the adjoining surfaces. If you are more assured of your skills, give yourself just an extra 1/16″ overall length.

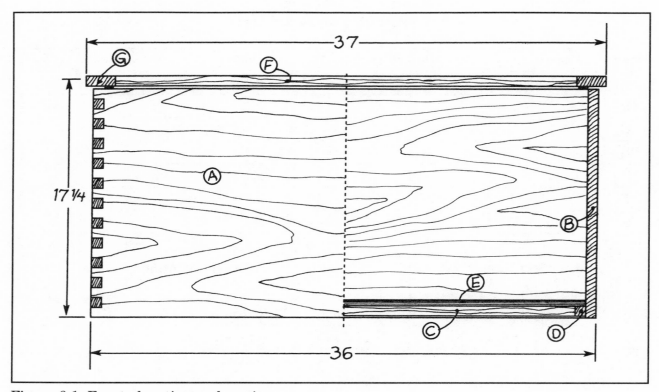

Figure 6.1. Front elevation and section

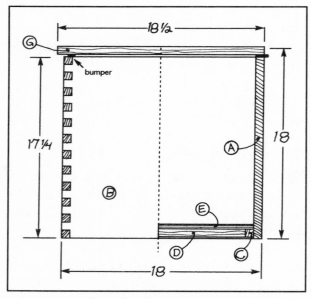

Figure 6.2. Side elevation and section

CUT FINGER JOINTS

Determine the position of each piece and mark its top edge. Number the corners 1 through 4 (each piece will have two numbers, one on either end). Next, as shown in Figure 6.3, draw a line across the grain 3/4″ (or ¹³/₁₆″) in from each end.

Clamp together the two pieces that form Corner 1 so their ends and their top and bottom edges are flush. On the end grain, lay out the fingers every 3/4″. Square these lines onto both faces. Mark with an X the waste material to be chopped away. Repeat the layout for each corner. Notice that the front and back have fingers at the top and bottom.

Again clamp Corner 1 together, but this time, as shown in Figure 6.3, shift the pieces one way or the other at least the thickness of the kerf of your saw. Two straight pieces of scrap stock along each cross-grain line will serve as both clamp blocks and a depth guide.

Careful study of Figure 6.3 will reveal the reason behind shifting the two pieces one way or the other. Clamping them to-

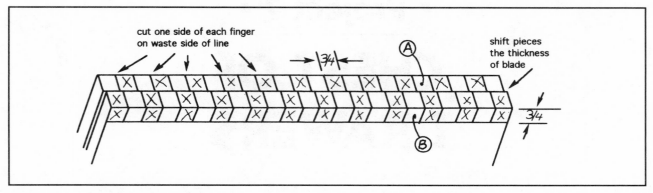

Figure 6.3. Finger joint detail

gether allows you to cut both pieces at the same time; shifting them allows you to cut on the waste side of each line.

• **Note:** Be very careful to cut every *other* pair of lines. Once you've cut one side of each finger, shift the pieces in the other direction to make the remaining cuts. This is important. Cutting on the wrong side of the line will make the fingers too narrow.

After you've made all the with-grain cuts, use a coping saw across the grain, well inside the line, to remove most of the waste. Then use a sharp 3/4" chisel to chop out the rest to the line.

Check the fit of each corner and make any necessary adjustments. The precision with which you made the cuts will determine how close the joints will fit. If you find gaps here and there, you can fill them with slivers of scrap later.

ASSEMBLY

Begin assembling the box by brushing glue on the fingers of both ends of the front and back. Work one end into place and then the other. Use enough clamps to draw the corners together, tapping them tight if necessary. Make sure the box is square before the glue sets.

When the glue has dried, sand the entire box thoroughly.

Cut the lid 19" wide by 34" long. Next join the 1 1/2" x 19" pieces to either end of the lid. Sand the faces smooth, then trim the lid to 18 1/2" wide.

Finally, glue and screw the cleats, Parts C and D, to the lower inside edges of the box. Cut and fit the bottom, but do not fix it into place. Remove it for ease of finishing.

FINISHING UP

Apply the finish of your choice.

Next, mount the continuous hinge (an assistant will be of help). Mounting the hinge on the underside of the lid—rather than on the back edge—will leave about a 3/16" gap at the back. Even this out with two small rubber bumpers at the front corners.

The left- and right-mount lid supports are each rated at 40–45 inch-pounds. Together they will keep the lid open at any position. Mount the supports according to the package instructions.

• **Note:** Spring-loaded hinges of this type are rated in "inch-pounds," i.e., how much weight the supports will hold. To determine approximate inch-pounds, multiply the weight of the lid by the front to back dimensions in inches, then divide the product by two. An 18"-deep lid weighing five pounds will require a pair of hinges rated at 45 inch-pounds each.

Install the optional handles about 4" from the top of the box.

▪ Project 7 ▪
CHEST OF DRAWERS

A good chest of drawers has adequate storage space for clothing. A better one allows for storage of other personal items. This one has both. Three deep drawers topped off by a shallower one are enclosed in the main case. Above them is a hutch with three small drawers and a shelf for many of the odds and ends kids will collect.

CONSIDERATIONS

Materials

The chest of drawers is made of solid pine, with $1/4''$ fir plywood for the back and drawer bottoms. The case and hutch are of $3/4''$ stock, as are the main drawer fronts. The sides and backs of the main drawers and the fronts and backs of the hutch drawers are $1/2''$ pine. Sides for the hutch drawers are $1/4''$ thick. You'll need about fifty board feet of pine and a sheet of plywood.

The only hardware used in this project are the brads or small nails you will use to tack on the backs, the $1\,1/4'' \times 8$ flathead wood screws for securing the top to the case, and the two sizes of knobs for the drawers. Of course, any kind of drawer hardware can be substituted.

No special hardware or treatment is given to the drawer slides. You can, however, make use of plastic guides or tape.

Project 7 Material List

Item	Description	Quantity	Thickness	Width	Length	Comments
A	Side	2	3/4″	18″	37″	solid pine
B	Top	1	3/4″	18 1/2″	26″	solid pine
C	Frame rail	1	3/4″	1 1/4″	24 1/2″	dovetail ends
D	Frame rail	4	3/4″	1 1/4″	24″	sliding dovetail
E	Frame rail	5	3/4″	1 1/4″	24″	
F	Frame end	10	3/4″	1 1/4″	15 3/4″	stub tenon ends
G	Toe kick	1	3/4″	3″	24″	rabbet ends
H	Back	1	1/4″	24 1/4″	34″	plywood
I	Hutch side	2	3/4″	8″	14 1/4″	
J	Top shelf	1	3/4″	8″	23″	sliding dovetail
K	Bottom shelf	1	3/4″	7 3/4″	23″	sliding dovetail
L	Divider	2	3/4″	7 3/4″	4 1/4″	
M	Rail	1	3/4″	3″	23″	rabbet ends
N	Back	1	1/4″	11 1/4″	23 1/4″	plywood
O	Drawer front	1	3/4″	6 3/8″	24″	3/8″ offset
P	Drawer back	1	1/2″	6″	23 1/4″	
Q	Drawer side	2	1/2″	6″	15 3/4″	
R	Drawer front	3	3/4″	8 1/8″	24″	3/8″ offset
S	Drawer back	3	1/2″	7 3/4″	23 1/4″	
T	Drawer side	6	1/2″	7 3/4″	15 3/4″	
U	Drawer bottom	4	1/4″	15 3/4″	22 3/4″	plywood
V	Drawer front, back	6	1/2″	3 3/4″	7″	
W	Drawer side	6	1/4″	3 3/4″	7 1/4″	
X	Drawer bottom	3	1/4″	7″	6 3/4″	plywood or solid
	Flathead screws	9	1 1/4″ x 8″			
	Flathead screws	14	1 1/2″ x 8″			
	Flathead screws	3	5/8″ x 6″			
	Knob, large	8	1 3/4″	diameter		
	Knob, small	3	1″	diameter		

Special Tools and Cuts

You will need these router bits:

    ¼″ straight

    ¼″ round-over

    ½″ dovetail

    ⅜″ rabbet bit with pilot

    ¾″ straight

    ogee or other decorative cutter

The case frames are assembled with stub-tenon joints and let into the case with a combination dado–sliding dovetail.

The toe kick, Part G, and the rail, Part M, have ¼″ x ½″ rabbet cuts on each end (forming a ¼″ x ¼″ tongue).

Sliding dovetail joints also hold the hutch shelves, Parts J and K, to the sides, and the hutch dividers, Parts L, to the shelves.

CONSTRUCTING THE CASE

Prepare Sides

First select the stock for the top and sides and glue it up into panels.

Cut the boards so that the panel blank is at least an inch wider and longer than the finished size.

When the side panels are dry, scrape away any squeezed-out glue and work the

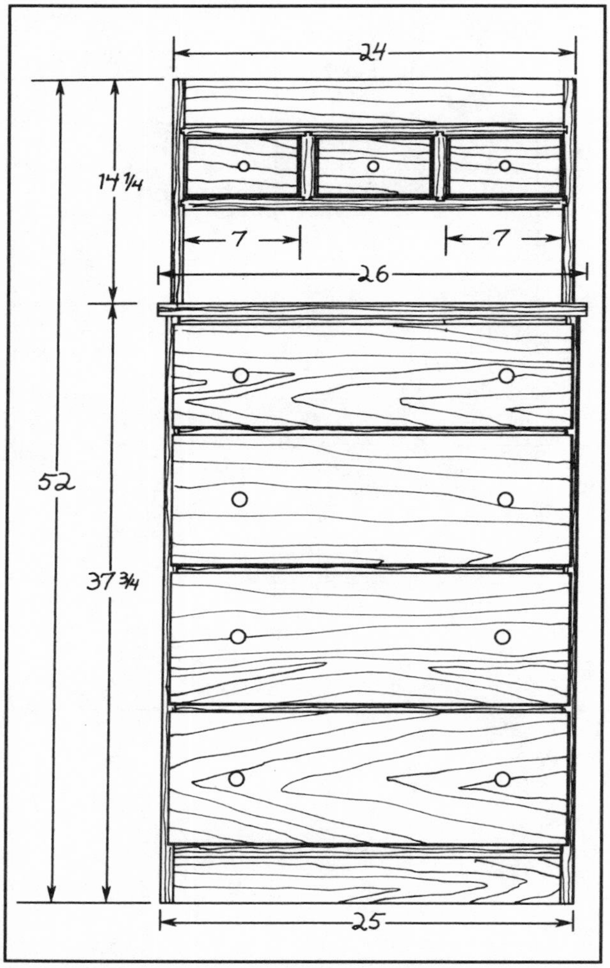

Figure 7.1. Front elevation

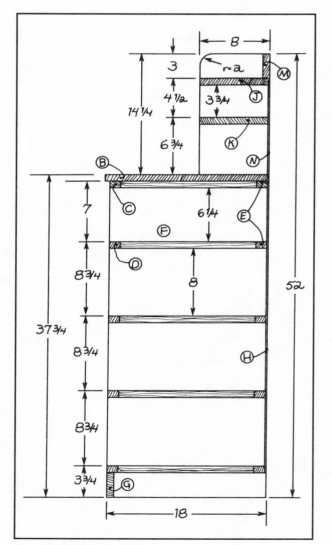

Figure 7.2. Section

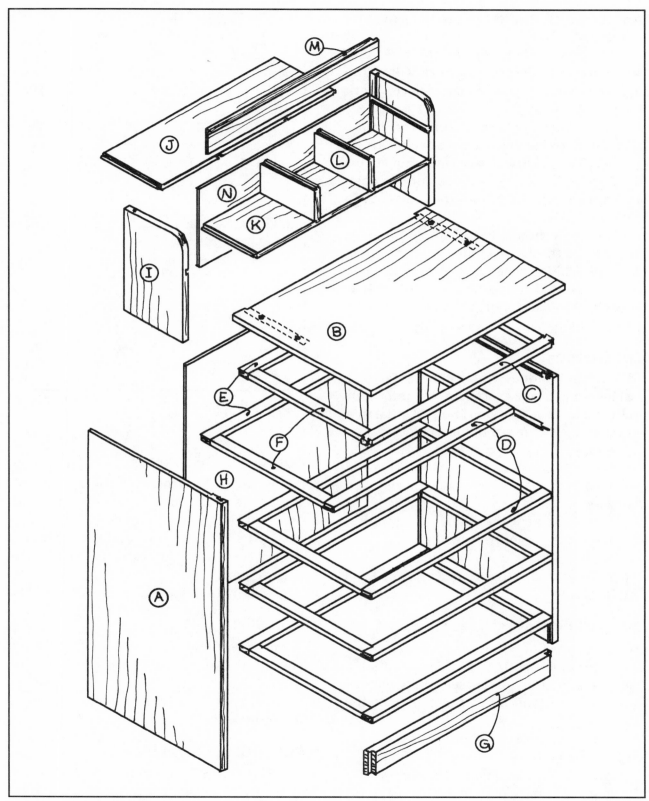

Figure 7.3. Exploded view

panels smooth. Rip the sides 18″ wide and cut them 37″ long.

Determine which will be the right and left sides. Then determine which will be the top and front edges of each piece. Mark them accordingly.

Cut a ³/₈″ x ¹/₄″ rabbet along the inside back edges to receive the case back, Part N.

Next, lay out the dadoes and rabbets for the frames. They are ³/₄″ wide and ¹/₄″ deep and stopped 1¹/₄″ from the front edge of the panel.

The frame fronts, Parts D, hold the sides together at the front by means of a sliding dovetail. The mortise is ¹/₄″ deep and must be in line with center of the stopped dado. It is itself stopped about ¹/₄″ from the front edge of the panel.

Cut Dadoes

To cut the dadoes and rabbets for the frames, chuck a ³/₄″ straight bit into your router and set it to a depth of ¹/₄″. Clamp a straightedge to the panel for a guide.

Before removing the guide after each cut, mark its position on the panel. This will be of use later, when cutting the dovetail mortises.

Once you've cut the dadoes and rabbets, chisel out the corners left by the bit.

Cut the ¹/₄″ x ¹/₄″ dado in each side for the toe kick, Part G. Cut the dado ¹/₂″ in from the front edge.

Cut Sliding Dovetail Mortises

Put a ¹/₂″ dovetail bit into the router and set it to the same depth as the dadoes. Clamp the guide to the marks set previously to orient the dovetail bit in the center of the dado.

Stop the mortise within ¹/₄″ of the front edge of the panel.

You will cut the dovetailed mortises for the topmost frame front, Part C, later.

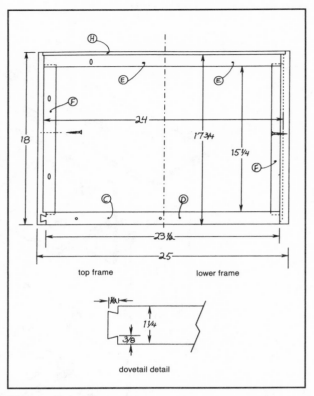

Figure 7.4. Plan view

Cut and Build Frames

Rip enough 1¹/₄″ stock for the frame rails and frame ends. Choose the best pieces for the front rails, Parts C and D.

Cut Part C 24¹/₂″ long and the remaining nine rails 24″ long. Cut the frame ends, Parts F, 15³/₄″ long.

Using a table-mounted router chucked with a ¹/₄″ straight bit set at ¹/₄″, mortise the ends of the front and back frame rails. Run the mortises in about 1³/₈″ (1⁵/₈″ for Part C). The mortises must be in the center of the stock.

Next cut a ¹/₄″ x ¹/₄″ tenon on each end of the frame ends.

Cut Sliding Dovetails

Designate each of the four front frame rails for a specific position in the case and mark it accordingly. Then cut and match each sliding dovetail with its mortise.

The fit should be snug, but not so tight you have to use excessive force. The front edges of the rails should be flush with—if not protruding 1/64″ beyond—the front edges of the sides.

Dovetail Top Front Rail

Cut the dovetailed tenons on the top front rail on the router table or by hand with a backsaw. Make sure the shoulder-to-shoulder distance is the same as those on the other rails.

Use the dovetails as patterns for their mortises in the sides. Chop out the mortises with a sharp chisel and check the fit.

Glue and clamp the frame members. Be sure the assembled frames are square.

Assemble Case

Because the sides are made of solid wood, and therefore susceptible to changes in humidity, only the dovetailed portions of the frames should be glued into place. To secure the frames to the side in the center, you will drive a 1 1/2″ x 8 flathead screw horizontally through a slotted pilot hole in the center of each frame end.

Working from the top, apply glue to either the dovetails or mortises and slip the frames into place.

It may be necessary to draw the sides tight to the frames with clamps before you drive the screws. Check the front for square and screw the frame ends to the panels.

Turn the case face down and check the fit of the back, Part H. Apply a bead of glue to the rails and down the sides. Use 5/8″ brads or other small nails to secure the back.

Now turn the case onto its back to install the toe kick, Part F. Coat the rabbeted ends of the toe kick and run a bead of glue along its upper edge. Slip it into place and clamp.

CONSTRUCTING THE HUTCH
Prepare Stock

Rip the hutch sides, Parts I, and top shelf, Part J, 8″ wide. The bottom shelf, Part K, and the dividers, Parts L, are 7 3/4″ wide. The rail, Part M, is 3″ wide. Cut all the pieces to length, remembering the tenons.

The shelves are joined to the sides, and the dividers to the shelves, with sliding dovetails. Lay out and cut the 1/4″-deep dovetailed dadoes through the entire width of the stock. Clamp a backup piece to the front edges to avoid tear-out.

Cut the dovetails in the ends of the shelves and dividers in the same manner as the frame rails in the case, testing the fit on scrap stock first. Because of the extra width of the boards, the fit should not be as snug as the rails. Rather, the joint should slide easily into place. If it must be forced without glue, *with* glue the pieces could seize before they can be brought into place.

Next cut the 1/4″ x 1/4″ dado for the back rail, Part M, and cut the tongues on the ends of the rail itself.

Lay out and cut the arcs in the sides.

▪ **Hint:** Although a radius of 2″ is suggested, it's not essential. Instead of locating the center of the circle and fumbling with a compass, use a jar lid or some other object of sufficient diameter lying about the shop.

Assemble Hutch

After making a dry assembly of the components, apply a thin layer of glue to one end or the other of the top shelf. Slip the shelf into its corresponding slot in the side. Apply steady, even pressure. Take care not to let the pieces seize. Make sure the edges are flush at the front.

Repeat the process for the bottom shelf.

Now apply glue to the dadoes in the opposite side. Ease the side onto the dovetails.

Apply glue to the dovetails on the dividers and slide them into place.

Glue and place the back rail, and apply clamps as necessary. Check for square.

Mount Hutch to Top

If you haven't done so already, work the top, Part B, to flatness. Cut it to width and length, then rout an ogee or other decorative cut around the front and sides.

Place the top on your workbench and the hutch assembly on top of it. Locate the hutch flush with the back edge of the top and in 1″ from each side. Lightly outline the "footprint" of the hutch on the top, then drill a pair of pilot holes within each of the outlines.

Drive four 1½″ x 8 flathead screws up through the top into the hutch assembly (Figure 7.3).

Now orient the assembly so that the hutch is resting on its face and the top is hanging over the edge of the workbench, perpendicular to the floor.

Use a ³/₈″ rabbet bit with a pilot set to a depth of ¼″ to rout a rabbet around the inside perimeter formed by the sides, top shelf and top. You will have to skip over the bottom shelf and the dividers, leaving small portions uncut. Chop out these portions with a chisel.

Now fit the back, Part N.

Apply a bead of glue to the shelves and the sides. *Do not* apply glue to the case top. Use brads to secure the back to the hutch portion of the assembly, but use three ⁵/₈″ x 6 flathead screws to secure the back to the case top. This allows you to separate the hutch from the top for finishing.

CONSTRUCTING THE DRAWERS

When you build drawers, consider the effects of humidity on them. Drawers made during humid periods will shrink. Those made during dry times could expand as the humidity rises—sometimes to the extent they cannot be opened, if they were made to fit too well. Personal judgment is the best guide for sizing drawers.

Main Drawers

The main drawers are offset ³/₈″ from the front of the case. The measurements given for the main drawers (and the hutch drawers, too) reflect ¼″ dovetails.

Rip the front, sides, and backs to the dimensions given, which allow ¼″ vertical clearance. Cut the backs 23¼″ long and the fronts 24″ long, allowing for ⅛″ clearance on each side.

Notice that the fronts are ¾″ longer than the backs but only ³/₈″ wider than the sides. Cut a ³/₈″ x ³/₈″ rabbet to form the lip around

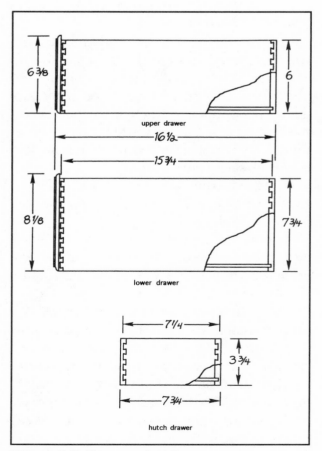

Figure 7.5. Drawer details

the top edge and the ends of the drawer fronts. A bottom lip is not necessary.

Cut the sides to length. Then rout the dovetails in the sides and in the fronts and backs of the pins.

Round over the top edges of the sides, then cut the $\frac{1}{4}'' \times \frac{1}{4}''$ grooves for the bottom. Locate the grooves so they run through the center of the lowermost dovetail and its corresponding pin.

Now, using a $\frac{1}{4}''$ round-over bit, round the edges of the drawer fronts. Leave a $\frac{1}{16}''$ fillet for visual interest.

Before assembling the drawers, sand the inside surfaces.

Hutch Drawers

The hutch drawers are different from the main drawers in that they are flush with the front edge of the hutch and they are stopped by the cabinet back.

The fronts and backs are $\frac{1}{2}''$ and the sides $\frac{1}{4}''$ thick. Cut the pieces to the same dimensions as the openings into which they will fit.

▪ **Hint:** Cut the drawer fronts from the same piece and mark their order. This will maintain the grain pattern across the front of the hutch.

Cut the tails and pins, then cut the grooves $\frac{1}{8}''$ deep for the bottoms.

The assembled drawers will likely be tight, as they are the same size as their openings. A block plane, a sander, and some patience will yield a perfect fit.

FINISHING UP

If desired, treat the front edges of the case sides and the hutch with a $\frac{1}{4}''$ round-over bit.

If you haven't already done so, disassemble the hutch from the case top. Then sand each component thoroughly, and apply the finish.

When the finish is dry, reassemble the hutch to the top. Drill a series of slotted pilot holes in the top frame (Figure 7.4). Align the hutch assembly and secure with $1\frac{1}{4}'' \times 8$ flathead screws.

Install the drawer pulls and insert the drawers.

• Project 8 •
STORAGE BED

The most versatile of beds expands its intended function to include storage. The storage bed contains ample storage space with four drawers in the headboard and as many as six large drawers in the platform.

The platform is designed to hold three drawers on either side for situations where the bed will be against a wall. The material list reflects that configuration. If the bed is intended for use in the center of the room, however, it will accommodate three additional drawers for double the storage capacity.

Project 8 Material List

Item	Description	Quantity	Thickness	Width	Length	Comments
A	Face frame rail	2	3/4″	2 1/2″	75 1/2″	
B	Face frame rail	2	3/4″	3″	75 1/2″	
C	Face frame stile	8	3/4″	2″	8 1/2″	stub tenon each end
D	Upper frame rail	2	3/4″	1 1/4″	75 1/2″	
E	Upper cross piece	2	3/4″	3″	37″	stub tenon each end
F	Upper cross piece	2	3/4″	4″	37″	stub tenon each end
G	Lower frame rail	4	3/4″	1 1/4″	24 3/8″	
H	Lower frame rail	2	3/4″	1 1/4″	24 3/4″	
I	Lower cross piece	2	3/4″	2 1/4″	37″	stub tenon each end
J	Lower cross piece	4	3/4″	1 5/8″	37″	stub tenon each end
K	Partition rail	4	3/4″	3″	39″	cut out bottom edge
L	Partition rail	4	3/4″	2″	39″	
M	Partition stile	8	3/4″	2″	6 1/4″	stub tenon each end
N	Drawer guide	4	3/4″	2″	35″	
O	Footboard	1	3/4″	24″	35 1/2″	
P	Footboard stile	2	3/4″	3″	24″	
Q	Side	2	3/4″	10″	52″	
R	Shelf	3	3/4″	10″	40 1/2″	sliding dovetails
S	Partition	2	3/4″	10″	12 1/4″	sliding dovetails
T	Shelf	2	3/4″	9 3/4″	12 1/4″	sliding dovetails
U	Apron	1	3/4″	11″	40″	
V	Leg	2	3/4″	3″	11″	
W	Rail	1	3/4″	3″	40 1/2″	rabbet each end
X	Back	2	1/4″	12 1/2″	12 1/2″	A/C plywood
Y	Mattress board	1	1/2″	39″	75 1/2″	A/C plywood or OSB
AA	Drawer front	3	3/4″	8 1/8″	23″	
BB	Drawer back	3	1/2″	7 3/4″	23″	
CC	Drawer side	6	1/2″	7 3/4″	15 3/4″	assumes 1/4″-long dovetails
DD	Drawer bottom	3	1/4″	15 3/4″	21 1/4″	
EE	Drawer front/ back	8	1/2″	5 1/2″	11 3/4″	

(Material List continued next page)

Project 8 Material List

Item	Description	Quantity	Thickness	Width	Length	Comments
FF	Drawer side	16	1/4″	5 1/2″	9 1/4″	assumes 1/4″-long dovetails
GG	Drawer bottom	4	1/4″	9″	11 1/2″	
	Flathead screws		1 1/4″ x 8″			
	Flathead screws		1 5/8″ x 8″			
	Flathead screws		2″ x 8″			
	Hex bolt	4	5/16″ x 2″			With 4 nuts and 8 washers
	Hex bolt	4	5/16″ x 1 1/4″			With 4 washers
	Threaded insert	4	5/16″ x 5/8″			
	Knob, large	3	1 3/4″			diameter
	Knob, small	4	1″			diameter

CONSIDERATIONS

A Word About Mattresses

The storage bed (as well as the convertible bunk beds and loft bed presented later) is sized to fit a standard 39″ x 75″ twin mattress. The U.S. Consumer Products Safety Commission recommends that a correctly sized mattress be used with any bed. If a mattress is too narrow or too short for the bed, a small child can become trapped between the mattress and the wall or headboard. Because mattresses come in different sizes (and a variety of compositions), I recommend you purchase, or at least pick out and measure, the mattress you intend to use and resize the plans if necessary.

Consider the composition of the mattress, the age and size of the child, and the number of years of expected service. Many inexpensive foam mattresses have short life spans and offer little support. A quality mattress, although more expensive, will last longer and offer more comfort than an inexpensive one.

Inquire about the warranty of a new mattress. Many mattresses are designed for use with a box spring or spring frame; use on a solid platform may void the warranty. Some mattresses, however, are designed for use on any base.

Materials

The storage bed uses about a hundred board feet of pine lumber. In addition, you will need sufficient 1/4″ A/C fir plywood for the drawer bottoms and a sheet of 1/2″ A/C or C/C fir plywood or 1/2″ ordered strand board (OSB—an alternative to plywood) for the mattress foundation.

To assemble the foundation frames you will need a good supply of 1 1/4″ x 8, 1 5/8″ x 8, and 2″ x 8 flathead screws.

The headboard is bolted to the platform with four 5/16″ x 2″ hex bolts with nuts and washers (or T-nuts). The footboard, however, requires a different treatment to conceal its fasteners. You will need four 5/16″ "threaded inserts" and four 5/16″ x 1 1/4″ hex bolts with washers.

Special Tools and Cuts

You will need these router bits:
   1/4″ straight bit

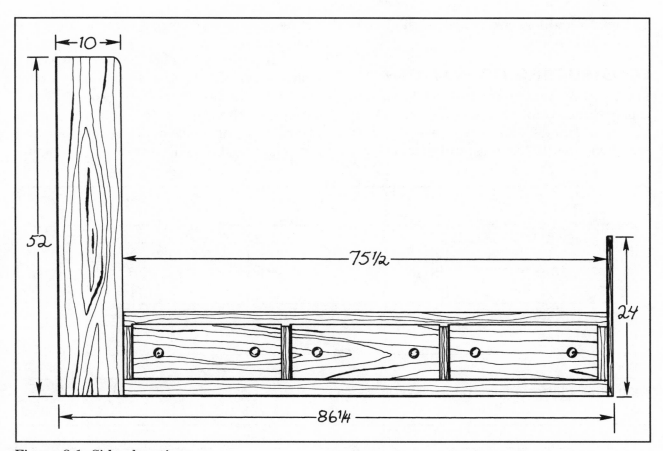

Figure 8.1. Side elevation

¹/₄″ round-over bit

¹/₂″ dovetail bit

You will also need a ¹/₂″ Forstner bit to bore flat-bottomed holes for the threaded inserts.

The storage bed is composed of three components: the platform, footboard, and headboard. At first glance the platform may look complicated, but broken down into individual components, it's a simple assembly.

Ten separate frames, themselves stub tenoned together, are glued and screwed to one another into a single unit.

The footboard is made of pine boards edged-glued together with a 3″ reinforcing stile on each end. Join the stiles to the main panel with biscuits or dowels.

The headboard uses sliding dovetails to join the shelves and partitions to the sides.

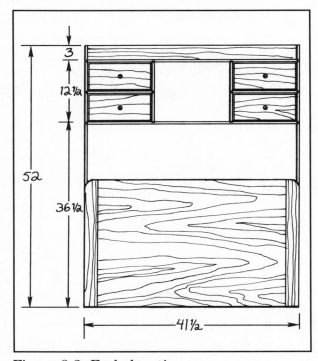

Figure 8.2. End elevation

The apron and legs are joined to the head-board with biscuits.

CONSTRUCTING THE PLATFORM

The platform is composed of an upper top frame, three bottom horizontal frames, four partition frames, and two face frames. Study Figures 8.3–8.8 carefully to get an understanding of how the frames relate to one another.

Cut the rails, cross pieces, and stiles, Parts A through N. Select the best stock for the face frames, Parts A, B, and C. Reference all the pieces to their respective frames, noting which are to be mortised and which to be tenoned.

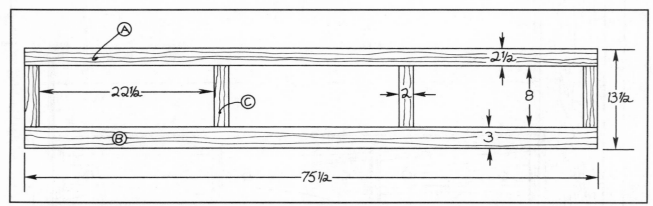

Figure 8.3. Platform face frame elevation

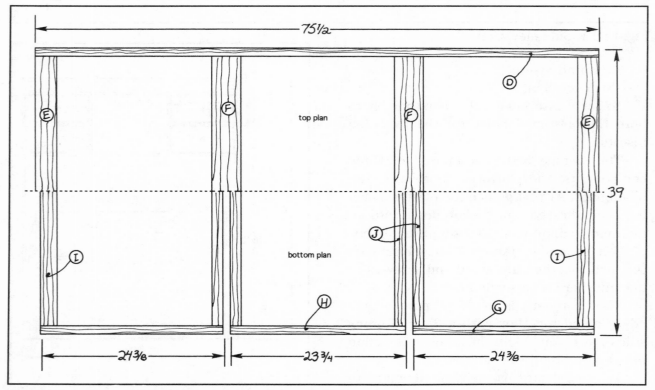

Figure 8.4. Plan of top and bottom horizontal frames

Assemble Frames

Lay the face frame stock on the bench and mark the position and orientation of the stiles and rails. Mortise the rails and cut the ¼" x ¼" tenons in the stiles.

• **Hint:** To save set-up time, lay out and cut the mortises and tenons in the other platform pieces now.

To assemble the face frames (Figure 8.3), apply glue to the bottom end of the tenons and slip them into their mortises in the bottom rail. Apply glue to the top ends of the tenons and bring the top rail into place. Clamp the frame across each stile and make sure each assembly is square.

Assemble the top and bottom frames (Figure 8.4). Notice that the outer bottom frames are opposites and unlike the center frame.

The four partitions are identical to one another. Before assembling them, however, make the cutouts in the bottom rails (Figure 8.5) so the frames will span any unevenness in the floor.

Assemble Platform

Begin assembling the platform by securing a partition to each end of the outer bottom frames. Apply glue, then clamp the partitions into place. Check the alignment: all adjoining surfaces should be flush. Drive four or five 1¼" x 8 flathead screws through each partition into the bottom frames.

Glue and clamp the center frame between the end assemblies. Check the alignment. Drive four or five 2" x 8 flathead screws through the frame into each partition.

Apply glue to the top edges of the partitions and set the top frame in place. Begin at one end and drive 1¼" x 8 screws down through the top frame into the partitions. Make sure the partitions are perpendicular to the top and bottom frames and the edges are flush all around.

Glue and clamp the face frames to the platform assembly. Drill pilot holes through the top and bottom horizontal frame rails, then drive 1⅝" x 8 flathead screws into the face frame from the inside.

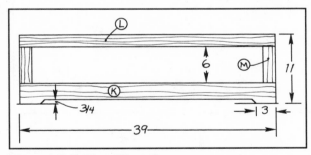

Figure 8.5. Partition frame

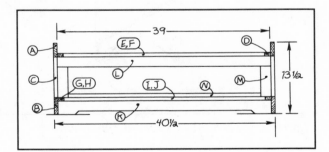

Figure 8.6. Platform section

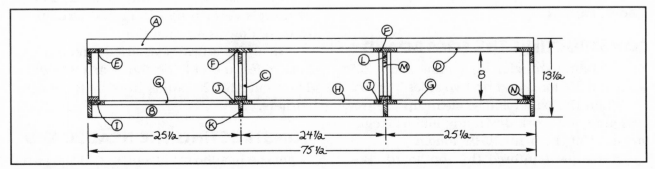

Figure 8.7. Platform section

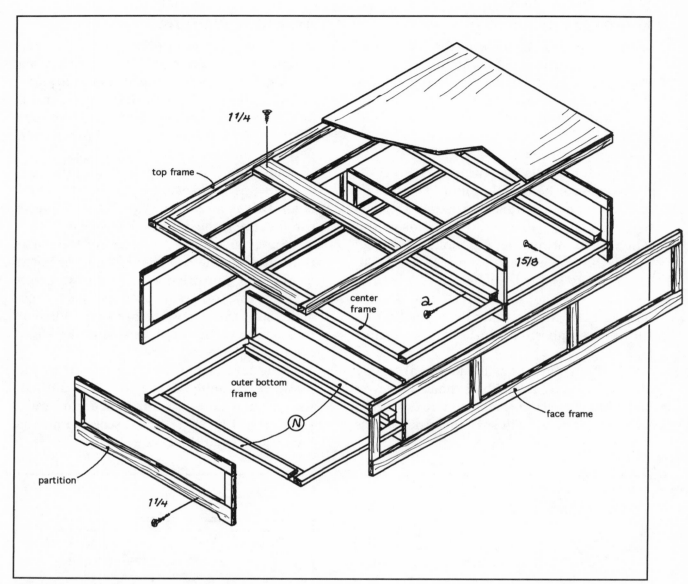

Figure 8.8. Exploded view of platform

Finally, glue and screw down the drawer guides, Parts N.

CONSTRUCTING THE FOOTBOARD

For the footboard, glue up a blank about 25" wide and 36" long, and rip two stiles 3" x 25".

When the panel is dry, clean up the excess glue and work down any major irregularities. Cut the blank 35½" long.

The stiles reinforce the footboard. Because the stiles are glued to end grain, the joint itself must be reinforced with biscuits or dowels. Use three #10 or #20 biscuits or four ¼" dowels on each side.

Once the stiles have dried, smooth out both sides and cut the footboard 24" wide. Then cut the 2" radius arcs in the upper corners.

CONSTRUCTING THE HEADBOARD

Begin the headboard by cutting all the parts to the dimensions given. Notice that the

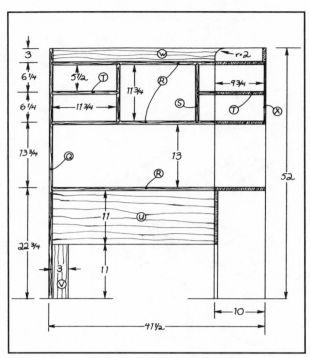

Figure 8.9. Headboard elevation and section

short shelves, Parts T, are ¼″ narrower than the sides, partitions, and long shelves. This is to accommodate the back, Part X.

The sides, shelves, and partitions interlock with sliding dovetails.

Lay out and cut the dovetailed slots ¼″ deep through the pieces, backing up the cuts to avoid tear-out.

Next cut the dovetailed tenons in the ends of the shelves and partitions. Make enough test cuts in scrap stock at least 10″ wide to satisfy a good fit. The pieces should slide together smoothly without binding. Do not make the fit so snug that you have to use force to slide the dovetails into position. Adding glue later will increase the friction, possibly so much that the pieces will seize on their way into place.

On the other hand, the fit should not be so loose that even with glue the joint will be sloppy.

Rout a ¼″ x ¼″ dado in the sides to accommodate the tongues on the ends of the

rail, Part W. The tenon on the rail is formed by a ¼″ x ½″ rabbet cut on the back face.

Lay out and cut a 2″ radius arc on the sides.

The apron, Part U, and the legs, Parts V, must be joined firmly to the sides and bottom shelf. Biscuits work well here, but a few moments of consideration of how these parts go together will reveal the need for quick and efficient assembly.

Cut slots for #10 biscuits in the sides, apron, and legs as shown in Figure 8.10.

Glue and insert biscuits into the ends of the apron, and apply a layer of glue to its upper edge. Then place the apron face down on the bench. Apply glue to the tenons on the bottom shelf.

Working quickly, bring the sides into place against the apron. Don't worry about getting the apron located precisely; it will align itself automatically against the bottom shelf. Instead, let the apron be off the mark ¼″ or so toward the bottom.

Now slide the bottom shelf into place. Turn the assembly over and make sure the front edge of the shelf is flush with the sides. Tap the apron upward against the shelf. Apply two or three clamps to hold the apron to the shelf, then clamp the sides to the apron.

Next, working from the back, glue up and slide the top shelf into place. Then slip in the rail, Part W. Clamp it to the shelf and clamp the sides across the back.

Insert the middle shelf, the partitions, and the short shelves. Clamp where necessary.

Rout a ³⁄₈″ x ¼″ rabbet around the inside perimeter of the drawer housings to receive the backs, Parts X. You will have to jump the router over the shelves, Parts T, and then use a chisel to chop out those areas the router didn't reach. Cut and fit the backs, but do not install them until you've applied the finish.

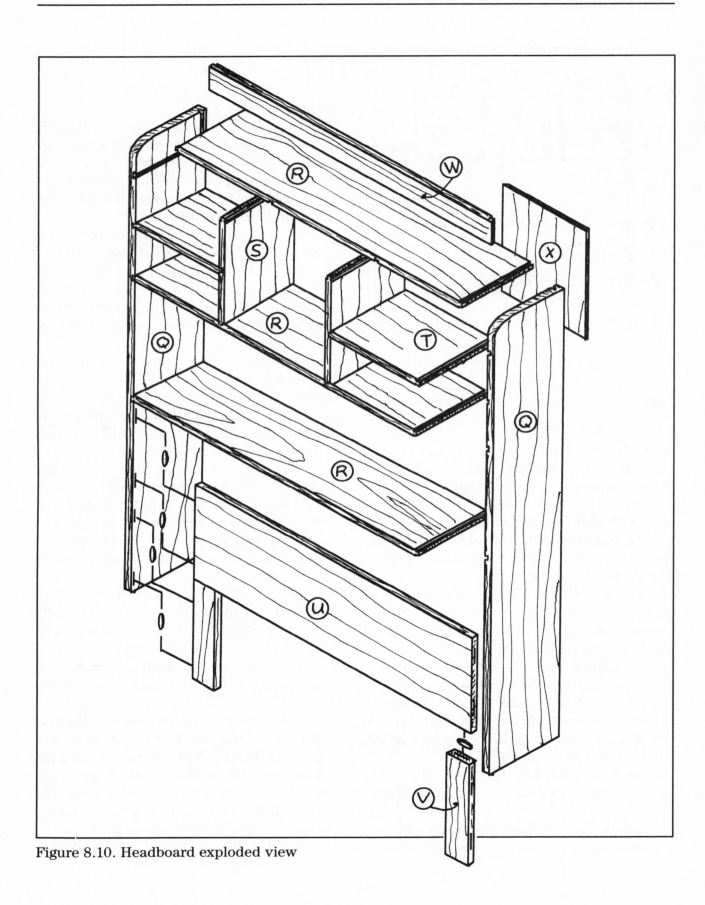

Figure 8.10. Headboard exploded view

Finally, using #10 biscuits, set and clamp the legs, Parts V, into place.

CONSTRUCTING THE DRAWERS

Platform Drawers

The platform drawers are made of solid pine and offset $3/8''$ from the face frame. The fronts are $3/4''$ thick, and the backs and sides are $1/2''$ thick. The drawers are joined with $1/2''$ machined dovetails, front and back. Bottoms are $1/4''$ plywood let into $1/4''$-deep grooves. Cutting the pieces to the given dimensions will allow $1/4''$ clearance top to bottom and $1/8''$ clearance on each side.

Cut a $3/8'' \times 3/8''$ rabbet in the top edge and each end of the fronts.

Round over the top edges of the backs and sides.

Cut the dovetails in the sides and the pins in the fronts and backs, then rout the $1/4''$ grooves to receive the bottoms. Locate the grooves so they run through the center

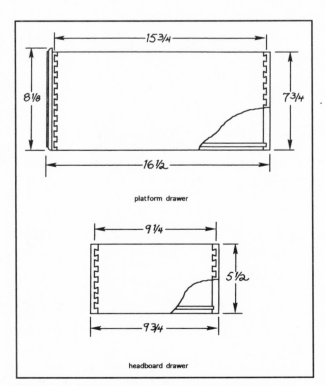

Figure 8.11. Drawer side elevations

of the lowermost dovetail and corresponding pin. That way the ends of the grooves won't show on the fronts and backs.

Now use a $1/4''$ round-over bit to treat the edges of the drawer fronts. Leave a $1/16''$ fillet for added detail.

Sand the inside surfaces before assembling the drawers.

Headboard Drawers

The headboard drawers are flush with the face of the headboard. The drawer fronts and backs are made of $1/2''$ stock and the sides of $1/4''$ stock. The bottoms are $1/4''$ plywood let into $1/8''$ grooves.

For a custom fit, cut the pieces so the assembled drawers will be the same size as their respective housings.

• **Note:** Discrepancies in the drawer housings are likely. Therefore, match each drawer to its own opening.

Cut the dovetails and pins, then rout the grooves for the bottoms. Sand the inside surfaces before assembling the drawers.

Sand smooth the outsides of the assembled drawers and check their fit. Use a block plane and sander to get the drawers to slide freely into place.

The back of the drawer housing serves as a stop for the drawers. How a drawer fits against the back affects how the front of the drawer relates to its opening.

Hold the back in place and push the drawer firmly against it. Study the margin around the drawer. It should be even from one side to the other. Carefully shave the back of the drawer to achieve a good fit at the front.

ASSEMBLING THE BED

The footboard is mounted to the platform with four $5/16'' \times 1 1/4''$ hex bolts with washers driven into threaded inserts in the footboard (Figure 8.12). The threaded insert requires a $1/2''$ diameter hole $5/8''$ deep.

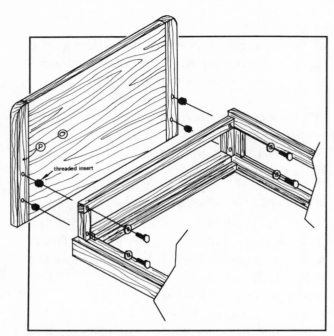

Figure 8.12. Footboard assembly detail

FINISHING UP

Disassemble the bed and thoroughly sand all the components. Apply the finish, then glue and tack the headboard backs into place. Install the drawer pulls.

Clamp the footboard to the platform and drill four $^1/_{16}$" diameter pilot holes through the platform and into the stiles of the footboard. (Don't go all the way through the footboard!)

Remove the clamps. Drill $^3/_8$" diameter holes through the pilot holes in the platform.

Use a $^1/_2$" Forstner bit to drill the flat-bottomed holes for the threaded insert. *Do not go deeper than $^5/_8$".* Drive the threaded insert into place.

Bolt the footboard to the platform.

Next, clamp the headboard to the platform and bore four $^3/_8$" diameter holes through the end portion and part V of the headboard. Bolt the headboard to the platform with four $^5/_{16}$" x 2" hex bolts with washers and hex nuts.

▪ **Note:** T-nuts anchored in the headboard can be substituted for the hex nuts.

Cut and fit the mattress board.

▪ Project 9 ▪
CONVERTIBLE BUNK BEDS

When two children must share a small bedroom, bunk beds are a good solution to a lack of space. Even if the room is large enough for a pair of twin beds on the floor, stacking them on top of one another opens up an enormous area.

Bunk beds come in two configurations: those that can be converted to twin beds and those that cannot. Convertible beds offer a substantial increase in usefulness. Some bunks simply separate into two beds, with no apparent change in design. That is, all eight posts are the same length, and the separated beds look like two halves of a set of bunks.

The convertible bunk beds described here are actually twin beds that can be easily converted to bunks. In the twin configuration, each bed has a tall headboard and a short footboard. In the bunk configuration, the lower bunk is fitted with the tall headboards, and the upper bunk with the shorter footboards.

▪ **Note:** Depending on the configuration, headboards can be footboards and vice versa. For the sake of clarity, *headboard* refers to the taller member, *footboard* to the shorter.

CONSIDERATIONS
Mattresses
Please read the important information under "A Word About Mattresses" at the beginning of Project 8.

Project 9 Material List

Item	Description	Quantity	Thickness	Width	Length	Comments
A	Long post	4	2¼″	2¼″	34″	
B	Short post	4	2¼″	2¼″	28″	
C	Side rail	4	¾″	5¼″	77″	1″ tenon each end
D	Ledger	4	¾″	3½″	77″	1″ tenon each end
E	End rail	4	¾″	5¼″	36¾″	join w/#20 biscuits
F	Headboard	2	¾″	14½″		join w/#20 biscuits
G	Footboard	2	¾″	8½″		join w/#20 biscuits
H	Slat	8	¾″	3½″	39″	
I	Mattress board	2	¼″	39″	75″	A/C plywood or OSB
J	Pegs	8			4″	¾″ dia. dowel
K	Rail (guardrail)	4	¾″	2½″	38″	join w/#10 biscuits
L	Stile (guardrail)	4	¾″	2½″	16¾″	
M	Ladder side	2	¾″	3¼″	52″	length approximate
N	Rung	4	¾″	3¾″	14½″	
	Connector bolt	8	3½″			
	Cross dowel	8				
	Connector bolt	4	2″			
	Cap nut	4				
	Ladder hook	1		pair		
	Flathead screws		1¼″ x 8″	as needed		
	Flathead screws	8	2″ x 8″			
	Screw buttons	8	⅜″	diameter		
	Plate-joinery biscuits	36	#20			
	Plate-joinery biscuits	8	#10			

Bunk Bed Safety

Apart from the cautions about mattress size, the U.S. Consumer Products Safety Commission recommends a number of other safety measures for bunk beds.

Guardrails should be on both sides of the upper bunk (and on both sides of a twin bed used by a young child as a first regular bed). Guardrails should be bolted or otherwise firmly attached to the bed. A rail that is inadvertently left off or that falls off during the night is of no use.

To ensure that a child cannot become trapped between the bed rail and the guardrail, that space should be no more than 3½". (This also applies to the space between rails at the head and foot of the bed.) Any guardrail should extend 5" above the mattress to prevent the child from rolling off the bed.

The CPSC has noted a number of accidents that occurred when a child, by kicking upwards from a lower bunk, dislodged the mattress foundation, bringing the whole works down upon himself (which can also happen when a child plays under a twin bed). Therefore, slats should be firmly attached to the rails.

Furthermore, the ladder should be secured to the bed so it can't slip while in use. The ladder that accompanies the bunk beds described here uses hooks to hold it in place.

Very young children should not be placed on the top bunk, and rough play on the beds should be discouraged.

Materials

Pine is well suited for these beds; you will need about seventy-five board feet of lumber. The posts are 2¼" x 2¼". In the absence of stock that thick, glue up three widths of ¾" stock. The pegs, which align and hold together the bunks, are ¾" diameter hardwood dowels.

Because these beds are convertible, rails and headboards have to be readily interchangeable. And, of course, the beds should be easily assembled and disassembled. To these ends, the design makes use of efficient knock-down (KD) hardware to secure the rails to the head- and footboards, and the guardrails to the rails.

Three-and-one-half-inch connector bolts run through the posts and are threaded into steel cross dowels inserted into the rails. The guardrail is secured to the rails with 2" connector bolts threaded into cap nuts. These items are available through a variety of mailing houses.

The connector bolts are exposed, but their low-profile heads have a statuary bronze finish that does not detract from the overall appearance of the beds.

▪ **Note:** The KD hardware described for use with the convertible bunk beds (and the loft bed, Project 10) was obtained by mail order from The Woodworkers' Store (21801 Industrial Blvd., Rogers, MN 55374-9514). Dimensions of hardware obtained from other sources may vary. Always get specialty hardware before beginning any project so you can make any necessary adjustment.

Also available by catalog are the hooks required to hold the ladder in place.

Special Tools and Cuts

You will need:

   4mm hex drive (for connector bolts)
   ¼" drill bit
   10mm drill bit
   ⅜" drill bit
   ¾" drill bit
   ¼" round-over bit

The rails at the head and foot of the beds are joined to the posts with #20 biscuits. The guardrail assemblies are joined with #10 biscuits.

The connector bolts and cross dowels provide the lateral strength to hold the rails to the posts. Shear strength, needed to support the weight of the bed rails and mattresses, comes from tenons on the ends of the rails, which bear within mortises chopped into the posts.

All edges are rounded with a ¼″ radius.

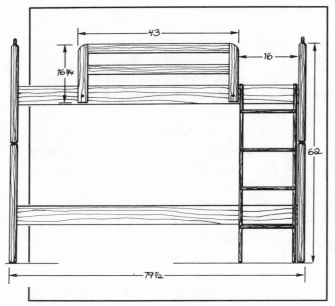

Figure 9.1. Side elevation

CONSTRUCTING THE HEADBOARDS AND FOOTBOARDS

Prepare Posts

If you can't find stock of sufficient thickness to make the posts, three ¾″ boards ripped 2⅝″ wide can be laminated for each leg. Each blank should be about 1″ longer than the finished post.

To ensure proper alignment of the stacked bunks, the posts must be square and of equal size. Once the posts are milled square, cut them to length.

The next step is to bore the holes for the pegs in the posts. Both ends of the short posts must be bored, but only one end of the long posts. (Regardless of the configuration, the tall headboards will always be on the floor.) Each hole must be centered in and perpendicular to the ends of the posts.

An effective way to bore the posts is with a radial-arm saw fitted with a drill chuck on the auxiliary arbor, with the arbor parallel to the table and fence. Push the post

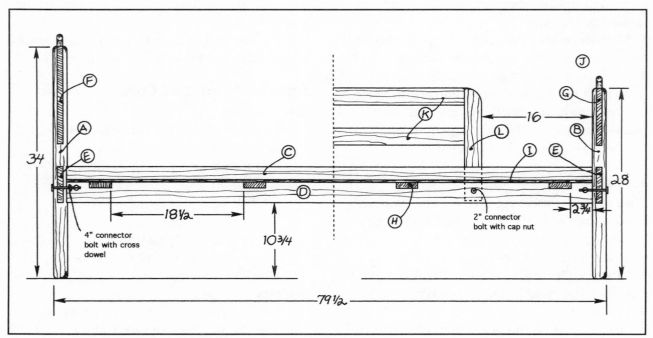

Figure 9.2. Section through ends

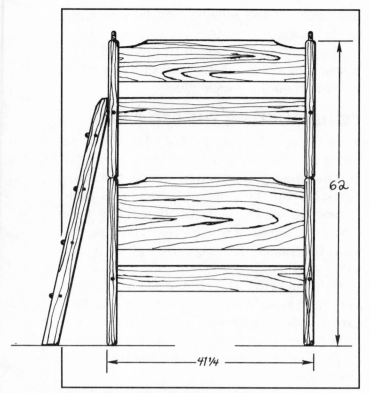

Figure 9.3. End elevation

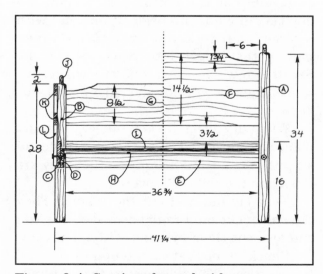

Figure 9.4. Section through sides

into the bit, and bore each hole at least 2⅛″ deep.

To help keep the posts oriented and to avoid confusion that can lead to cutting a

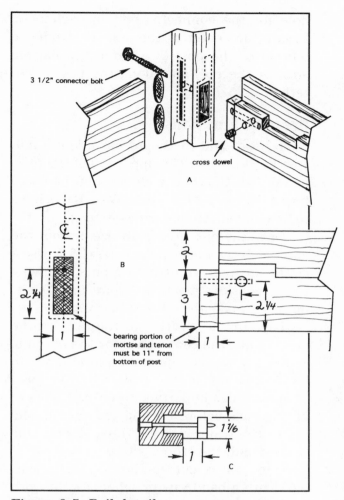

Figure 9.5. Rail details

mortise into the wrong face of a post, mark each post and its orientation.

Next lay out the position of the bed rails and their 1″ x 3″ mortises directly onto the posts, as shown in Figure 9.5.

Use a 1″ bit to bore out most of the waste, then finish the mortise with a chisel.

▪ **Note:** Intentionally make these mortise and tenon joints a little loose to facilitate assembly and disassembly. It's important, however, that the bearing portion of the mortise is 11″ from the bottom of each post (and the bearing portion of the tenon must be in the same place relative to the bottom edge of the rail).

After chopping the mortises, drill a ⅜″

hole for the connector bolt in each post. Locate the center of the hole 13″ from the bottom of the post (2¼″ from the bottom edge of the rail) and along the post's centerline.

Prepare End Rails

Each head- and footboard has a lower rail, Part E, 5¼″ wide. The upper rail of the footboard, Part G, is 8½″ wide; that of the headboard, Part F, is 14½″ wide. Parts F will have to be glued up from narrower stock.

Once the rails are cut to size, lay out the cutouts in the upper rails, Parts G & F. Use a cardboard pattern of the cutouts following the dimensions given in Figure 9.4. Don't, however, make the cutouts just yet.

Lay out the position of the rails on the posts. Mark the centerlines for the biscuits. You will have to adjust the plate joiner to locate the rail in the center of the post. Therefore, it's important to cut the slots in all the rails before cutting the slots in the posts. The wider rails get three #20 biscuits in each end, the others get two.

Once you've cut the slots, make the cutouts with a band saw or saber saw. Smooth out and round over the edges (not the ends) with a ¼″ router bit. Also round all the edges of the posts, including the tops and bottoms. Sand the pieces to 150-grit. Do not sand away the reference marks for the rails.

Assemble Headboards and Footboards

Glue in the biscuits and attach the rails to the posts. Check that the rails are in their correct positions vertically. Clamp the assemblies securely until dry.

Cut eight ¾″ diameter pegs 4″ long. Chamfer both ends and cut a V-groove about ¾″ down from the top of each peg. Brush a small amount of glue inside the holes at the tops of the posts. Don't apply glue to the pegs. Doing so will cause excessive squeeze-out, difficult to remove from the end grain of the posts.

Insert 2″ of the pegs into the holes. The holes should be a little deeper than 2″ to provide room for excess glue.

CONSTRUCTING THE BED RAILS

Each bed rail is composed of two parts, the outer rail, Part C, and the inner ledger, Part D. The ledger is notched to receive the slats, Parts H. Rip the rails and ledgers to their respective widths and cut them 77¼″ long (the extra length is to allow for trimming the ends flush once the ledgers are glued to the rails).

Working from the center of each ledger, lay out the notches. Cut them on a radial-arm saw or with a saber saw.

▪ **Note:** Do not notch the ledgers so close to the ends that the notches interfere with the tenons.

Glue and screw (1¼″ x 8) the ledgers to the inside of the rails, keeping them as flush as possible at the bottom. If the bottoms don't readily line up, begin at one end with a screw and work your way to the other, pulling the ledger into place as you go. Seven screws in each rail are sufficient; space them evenly for the sake of appearance.

When dry, clean up any squeeze-out and plane the bottom edges so they are flush and smooth. Then trim the ends so that they are flush and the rail is 77″ overall.

Next lay out and cut the tenons. They are easily cut on a radial-arm saw, but you can also cut them by hand with a backsaw.

Check to see that each tenon fits into all the mortises. This will ensure that the rails can be interchanged.

Lay out and drill the holes in the rails for the cross dowels and connector bolts (Figure 9.5B). Drill the 10mm holes for the cross dowels first, taking care that they are perpendicular to the surface. Then drill the ¼″

holes into the rail ends for the connector bolts.

Round the outside edges and the bottom inside edges of the rails with a ¼″ round-over bit.

CONSTRUCTING THE GUARDRAILS

The convertible bunk beds are equipped with two guardrails for the upper bunk. Rip enough 2½″ stock for the rails and stiles and cut the pieces to length.

Join the rails to the stiles with #10 biscuits.

When the guardrails are dry, smooth up the joints. Then cut a 2″ radius arc at each upper corner. Round over all edges with a ¼″ bit.

Select two bed rails for the upper bunk. Clamp a guardrail to each of the bed rails, locating it 16″ from the shoulder of the tenon and up ½″ from the bottom of the rail.

Bore a ⅜″ hole 2¼″ up from the bottom and along the centerline of each guardrail stile for the connector bolts.

CONSTRUCTING THE LADDER

To build and fit the ladder, you need to first assemble and stack the beds. It's also a good

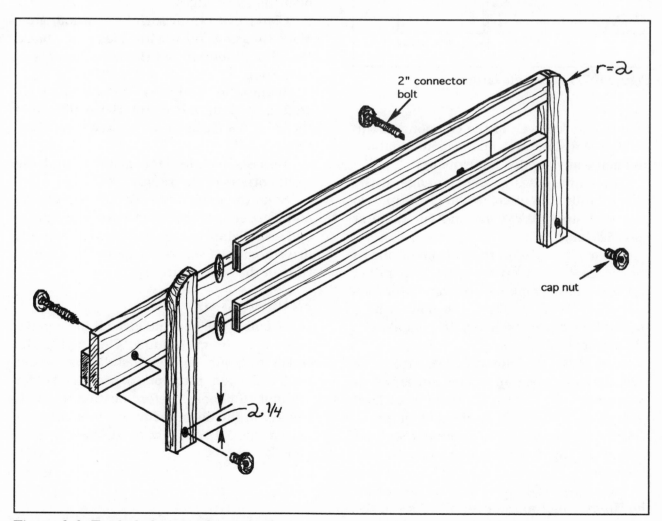

Figure 9.6. Exploded view of guardrail

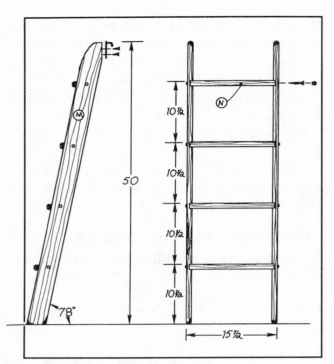

Figure 9.7. Ladder elevations

time to check the fit of the components (including the slats and mattress foundation) and make any needed adjustments.

The ladder rises to the top edge of the upper bunk rail at a 78° angle. Rip two pieces of stock 3¼″ wide and cut them at least 52″ long.

Cut a 12° angle on the bottom of one of the pieces. Lean the piece against the rail of the upper bunk, making sure the bottom sits evenly on the floor. Mark the point where the ladder side meets the rail, then make the 12° level cut at the top.

Next make the plumb cut 90° from the level cut. The position of this cut is not as important as its length. It should be at least as long as the shank of the ladder hook. Next cut a gentle curve around the front edge at the top. Use this side as a pattern for the other.

Lay out—but do not cut—the dadoes for the rungs. Then round over all edges of the sides except those of the plumb cuts.

Place the ladder sides against the rail of the upper bunk and mark the position of the ladder hooks.

▪ **Note:** The hooks are to keep the ladder from slipping away from the bed, not to support it; the ladder should remain firmly on the floor.

Now chisel out the mortises for the hooks.

Use a radial-arm saw fitted with a dado head, or a router with a ¾″ straight bit, to cut the dadoes in the ladder sides.

To make the rungs, cut four pieces 3¾″ x 14″, and bevel the back edges to match the incline of the sides. Then round over the front edges.

Clamp everything together without glue. Make the rungs flush with sides at the back. Pencil in a tight arc on the front corners of each rung.

While the ladder is still clamped together, predrill and counterbore the holes for the 2″ x 8 flathead screws and screw buttons.

Disassemble the ladder, and round the front corners of the rungs.

Sand the ladder components thoroughly and reassemble, this time with glue in the dadoes. Clamp the assembly together and drive home the screws. Remove the clamps. Glue in the screw buttons.

FINISHING UP

Disassemble the bed and give all the components a thorough sanding. Then apply the finish of your choice. Install the ladder hooks. Do not attempt to use the ladder without the hooks. Before putting the mattresses on the beds, secure each of the slats with a single 1¼″ x 8 flathead screw in each end.

▪ Project 10 ▪

LOFT BED

Like the bunk beds, the loft bed is a space saver, but with a difference: the loft bed is for one child. It boosts the mattress high above the floor, leaving space beneath it for the chest of drawers (Project 7) and the study desk (Project 13), with enough room left over for a secret hideout.

Each end frame incorporates a built-in ladder. You could also install a row of pegs along the inside of the back rail to hang hats and coats.

CONSIDERATIONS

The height of the loft bed precludes its use in a room with a ceiling less than seven and a half feet above the floor. A ceiling of eight feet or higher is ideal.

The same considerations for mattresses and safety apply to the loft bed as to the storage and bunk beds. See the respective sections in those chapters for important information.

Materials

Pine works just as well for the loft bed as it does for the other beds in this book. You will need about forty-five board feet of lumber and about twenty linear feet of 1″ dowel stock for the ladder rungs. The posts are 2¼″ x 2¼″ and can be of solid or laminated stock. The posts are topped with ¾″ diameter hardwood pegs.

Along with the square posts, the end frames also use 1½″ x 3½″ and 1½″ x 2¼″ members. Like the posts, they can be solid or laminated.

The bed rails and guardrails are the same as those used in the bunk beds. Refer to Figures 9.3–9.6 for details.

The loft bed uses 3½″ connector bolts and steel cross dowels to secure the rails, stabilizer bar, Part H, and braces, Parts I, to

Project 10 Material List

Item	Description	Quantity	Thickness	Width	Length	Comments
A	Post	4	2¼"	2¼"	70"	
B	End rail	4	1½"	3½"	36¾"	join w/#20 biscuits
C	Stile	2	1½"	2¼"	64"	2" tenon each end
D	Rung	12			18¼"	1" dia. dowel
E	Peg	4			4"	¾" dia. dowel
F	Side rail	2	¾"	5¼"	77"	1" tenon each end
G	Ledger	2	¾"	3½"	77"	1" tenon each end
H	Stabilizer bar	1	1½"	3½"	76¼"	¼" tenon each end
I	Brace	2	1½"	2¼"	34"	length approximate
J	Slat	4	¾"	3½"	39"	
K	Mattress board	1	½"	39"	75"	A/C plywood or OSB
L	Rail (guardrail)	4	¾"	2½"	38"	join w/#20 biscuits
M	Stile (guardrail)	4	¾"	2½"	16¾"	
	Connector bolt	10	3½"			
	Cross dowel	10				
	Connector bolt	4	2"			
	Cap nut	4				
	Flathead screws		1¼" x 8"			
	Plate-joinery biscuits	6	#20			
	Plate-joinery biscuits	8	#10			

the end frames. For additional information on the hardware used in the loft bed, refer to the information in Project 9.

Special Tools and Cuts

You will need:
    4mm hex drive (for connector bolts)
    ¼" drill bit
    10mm drill bit
    ¾" drill bit
    1" drill bit
    ¼" round-over bit

The end rails, Parts B, are plate-joined to the posts with #20 biscuits in pairs.

▪ **Note:** If you prefer, the end rails and posts can be mortised and tenoned rather than plate-joined. Make the tenons 1" x 3" and about 1¾" long and pin them with ¼" dowels (or run them all the way through and wedge them). Of course, if you choose this method, you must add the length of the tenons to the rails.

The guardrails are joined with #10 biscuits.

The connector bolts and cross dowels provide the lateral strength to hold the bed rails to the posts. Shear strength, needed to support the weight of the bed, comes from 1″-long tenons on the ends of the bed rails, which bear within mortises chopped into the posts. The stabilizer and diagonal braces are attached to one another and to the end frames with connector bolts and cross dowels. The ends of these members have tenons 1/4″ long.

All edges are rounded with a 1/4″ radius.

PREPARATION

If you can't find stock of suitable dimensions for the posts and rails, rip enough 3/4″ stock for laminating. Remember to give extra width and length to the individual pieces so you can mill the blanks into shape.

Cut the posts, Parts A, to length, then bore 3/4″ diameter holes 2″ deep in the tops for the pegs.

Cut the end rails, Parts B, 36 3/4″ long and the stiles, Parts C, 64″ long.

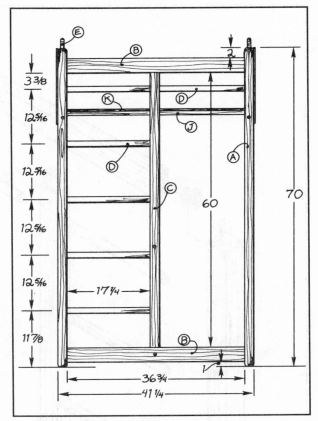

Figure 10.2. End elevation

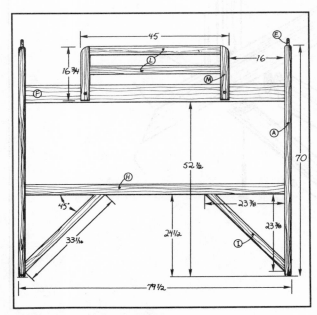

Figure 10.1. Side elevation

Mark each piece in relation to its position in the frame.

CONSTRUCTING THE END FRAMES

Begin with the posts. Lay out and cut the 1″ mortises for the bed rails. For details, refer to Figure 9.5 in Project 9. The bearing portion of the mortises should be 52 3/4″ from the bottom of the posts. Next bore the 3/8″ diameter holes for the connector bolts through the posts.

Now lay out the positions of the top and bottom rails, Parts B, on the posts. Then mark the centerlines for the biscuits on the posts and the rails. Each rail end has two #20 biscuits side by side, so you will need centerlines on both faces of each piece (Figure 10.3).

Cut the slots in the ends of the rails first.

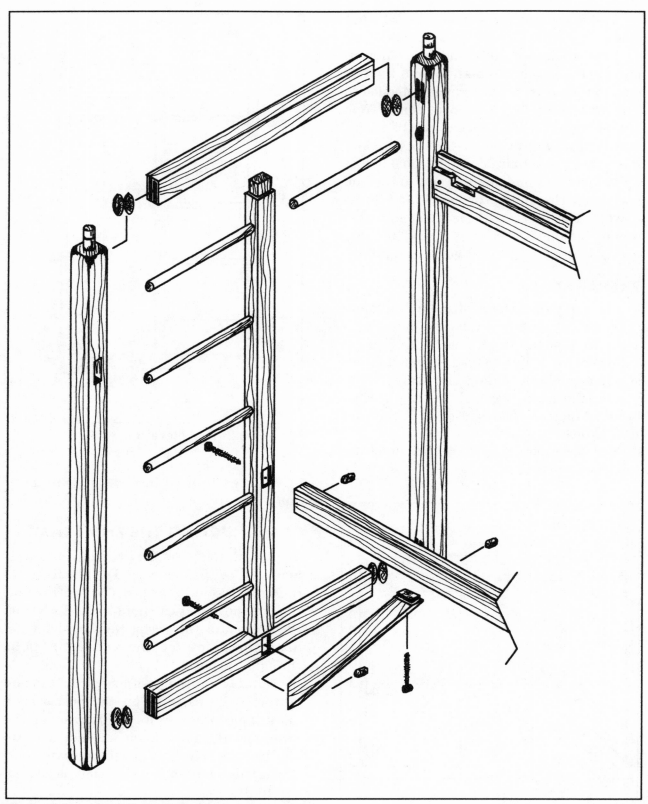

Figure 10.3. Partial exploded view

Set the plate joiner as you would to cut a slot in the center of a piece of ¾" stock. Make the first cut, then turn the rail over for the second. Repeat the process until all the end slots are cut.

Raise the bit ⅜". Make a couple of test slots in a piece of 2¼" scrap stock to make sure the final slots will align with those in the ends of the rails. Then cut the slots in the posts, again, working from each face.

Now lay out the center stiles, Parts C, and their mortises in the rails. Make the mortises 1" wide by 1¾" long and 2¹⁄₁₆" deep.

Cut the tenons in the stiles 1" x 1¾" x 2" long.

Now lay out the holes for the rungs. Place the outside posts (the ones that would be away from the wall) alongside their respective stiles on the bench. With their opposing surfaces facing up, align them relative to the rails. Then lay out the rungs. Don't forget to lay out the single rung opposite the ladder. This rung decreases the space between the mattress and the top rail. Do not bore the holes yet.

The edges of all the components of the end frames are rounded over with a ¼" bit. The procedure must be done in stages, however, some before and some after assembly. Do the posts first, including the tops and bottoms. Next do the stiles. Stop the cuts just short of the ends.

Now bore the 1" diameter holes for the rungs. Use a drill press to ensure accuracy. Make the holes ½" deep.

Cut the rungs, Parts D, 18¼" long.

Begin the end assembly by first gluing the rails to the stiles. Make sure they are clamped tightly and squarely. Remove any squeeze-out from the joints, then finish rounding over the edges.

Now, working quickly, brush glue inside the holes for the rungs, and apply glue to the biscuits and ends of the rails. Place the rungs into position in the stile and bring all the components together. Make sure everything is in alignment. Clamp the assembly. Don't forget the single rung opposite the ladder.

CONSTRUCTING THE BED RAILS
Each bed rail is composed of two parts, the outer rail, Part F, and the inner ledger, Part G. The ledger is notched to receive the slats. Rip both pieces to their respective widths and cut them 77¼" long. The extra length is to allow for trimming the ends flush once the ledgers are glued to the rails.

Working from the center of each ledger, lay out the notches. Cut them on a radial-arm saw or with a saber saw.

▪ **Note:** Make sure the notches at each end of the rails will not interfere with the tenons.

Glue and screw (1¼" x 8) the ledgers to the inside of the rails, keeping them flush at the bottoms. If the bottoms don't readily line up, begin screwing at one end and work your way to the other, pulling the ledger into place as you go. Seven screws in each rail are sufficient; space them evenly for the sake of appearance.

When the glue is dry, clean up any squeeze-out, and plane or sand the bottom edges so they are flush and smooth. Now, measuring from the center, trim the ends so the rails are 77" long.

Next lay out and cut the tenons. Use a radial-arm saw or cut them by hand with a backsaw.

Round the outside edges and the bottom inside edges of the rails with a ¼" round-over bit.

CONSTRUCTING THE GUARDRAILS
The loft bed is equipped with two guardrails. For details, refer to Figure 9.6 in Project 9. Rip enough 2½" stock for the rails and stiles, and cut the pieces to length.

Join the rails to the stiles with #10 biscuits.

When the guardrails are dry, smooth up the joints. Then cut a 2″ radius arc at each upper corner. Round over all edges with a ¼″ bit.

Clamp a guardrail to each bed rail, locating it 16″ from the shoulder of the tenon and up ½″ from the bottom of the rail.

Bore a ⅜″ hole 2¼″ up from the bottom and along the centerline of each guardrail stile for the connector bolts.

CONSTRUCTING THE STABILIZING SYSTEM

The stabilizing system is composed of the stabilizer bar, Part H, and the braces, Parts I.

The stabilizer bar is 76¼″ long and the braces are approximately 34″ long.

Lay out the two mortises in each end frame and the two mortises on the bottom edge of the stabilizer (Figure 10.3 and 10.4).

Round over the edges of the stabilizer and braces before chopping the mortises.

The tenons on the stabilizer are straightforward, formed with a ¼″ x ¼″ rabbet on all sides. The tenons of the braces are the same size but, because of the angles, require a bit more attention when laying them out. The long-point-to-long-point distance between the shoulders on the braces is 33¹⁄₁₆″. Cut the braces to length, then cut the tenons with a backsaw.

Bore ⅜″ holes through the mortises in the end frames as shown. Notice in Figure 10.4 the connector bolt that joins the brace to the end frame is not centered vertically in the mortise. Notice also the connector bolt that joins the brace to the stabilizer bar intersects the brace at a 45° angle. A ¾″ diameter pocket must be bored into the brace so the connector bolt will seat squarely. Complete the hole through the tenon with a ⅜″ bit.

Lay the stabilizer and braces face down

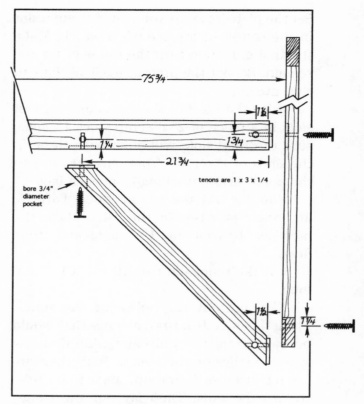

Figure 10.4. Brace details

on the bench and put them together. Mark the location of the connector bolts and cross dowels. Drill ¼″ diameter holes for the connector bolts and the 10mm holes for the cross dowels.

ASSEMBLY AND FINISHING UP

Bolt the braces to the stabilizer, then bolt this assembly to the end frames. Keep the bolts fairly loose so the end frames will lean out far enough to allow placement of the bed rails.

Bring the bed rails into place. Tighten all connector bolts and check the fit of each of the parts, including the slats and mattress board.

Disassemble the bed. Sand it thoroughly, then apply the finish.

Before placing the mattress foundation, secure each of the slats with a 1¼″ x 8 flathead screw in each end.

· Project 11 ·
TYKE'S TABLE

By the age of two, a child's interest in "doing" has begun to develop in earnest. A busy child needs a place to work. Here is a little table just right for everything from finger paints to tea and cookies. A drawer is located in each end of the table; there is no front or back.

CONSIDERATIONS
Materials

How you plan to use the tyke's table will have bearing on what materials you'll use. Pine is a good all-around wood. Oak will take more abuse, but some people might

Project 11 Material List

Item	Description	Quantity	Thickness	Width	Length	Comments
A	Leg	4	1½″	1½″	23¼″	
B	Long apron	2	¾″	5″	26¾″	
C	End apron spacer	4	¾″	3½″	2⅞″	
D	End apron rail	4	¾″	¾″	16¾″	
E	Kicker	1	¾″	1¼″	26¼″	stub tenon ea. end
F	Drawer runner	2	¾″	2″	26¼″	stub tenon ea. end
G	Drawer guide	4	¾″	¾″	10″	
H	End stretcher	2	¾″	2″	17″	
I	Center stretcher	1	¾″	2″	27¼″	
J	Top	1	¾″	20″	30″	2″ rad. on corners
K	Drawer front	2	¾″	3⅝″	11½″	⅜″ offset
L	Drawer back	2	½″	3¼″	10¾″	
M	Drawer side	4	½″	3¼″	13″	assumes ¼″ tails
N	Drawer bottom	2	¼″	10¼″	13″	plywood
	Knob	2	1¾″			dia. wood or other
	Flathead screws	10	1″ x 6″			for cabinetmakers' buttons
	Flathead screws	8	1¼″ x 6″			for drawer guides
	Cabinetmakers' buttons	8				

wonder at the expense if they think it will get too much abuse. An alternative is to cover the top with plastic laminate.

The legs are 1½″ square. If you can't find stock of sufficient dimension for the legs, laminate two pieces of ¾″ stock.

The drawers are ⅜″ offset. The fronts are made of ¾″ stock and the sides and back are ½″ stock. The drawer bottoms are ¼″ plywood.

You will need about twenty board feet of lumber, excluding the plywood.

Special Tools and Cuts
You will need these router bits:
¼″ straight

¼″ round-over
⅜″ rabbet
½″ dovetail

The tyke's table uses mortise and tenon joinery. The tenons on the aprons are mitered to make use of their full length. The center stretcher is through-tenoned and wedged into the end stretchers.

The drawers are joined with ½″ dovetail joints.

MILLING THE PIECES
Rip the long aprons, Parts B, 5″ wide.

To make the end aprons cut four spacers, Parts C, 3½″ wide and about 4″ long. Rip the rails, Parts D, ¾″ wide and about 16″ long.

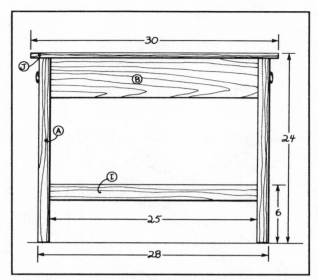

Figure 11.1. Front elevation

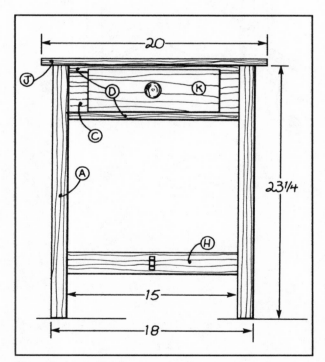

Figure 11.2. End elevation

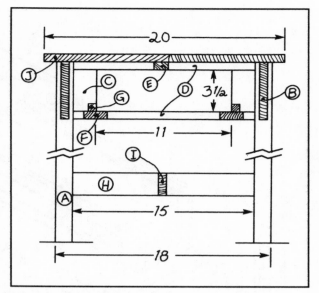

Figure 11.3. Section

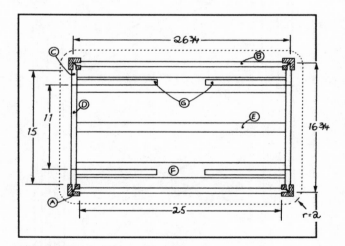

Figure 11.4. Plan view

Glue the rails to the spacers, leaving 11″ between the spacers.

Cut the legs 23¼″ long. Determine each one's position in the table and mark it accordingly. Do the same with each apron.

Lay out the apron mortises in each leg, following the dimensions given in Figure 11.6. Use a drill press with a ¼″ bit to take out most of the waste, and finish the job with a chisel. Or use a ¼″ straight bit in a table-mounted router, taking small bites at a time, creeping up on the desired depth.

Cut the tenons on the aprons. The distance between the shoulders is 25″ on the long aprons and 15″ on the end aprons. When laying out the end aprons, work from

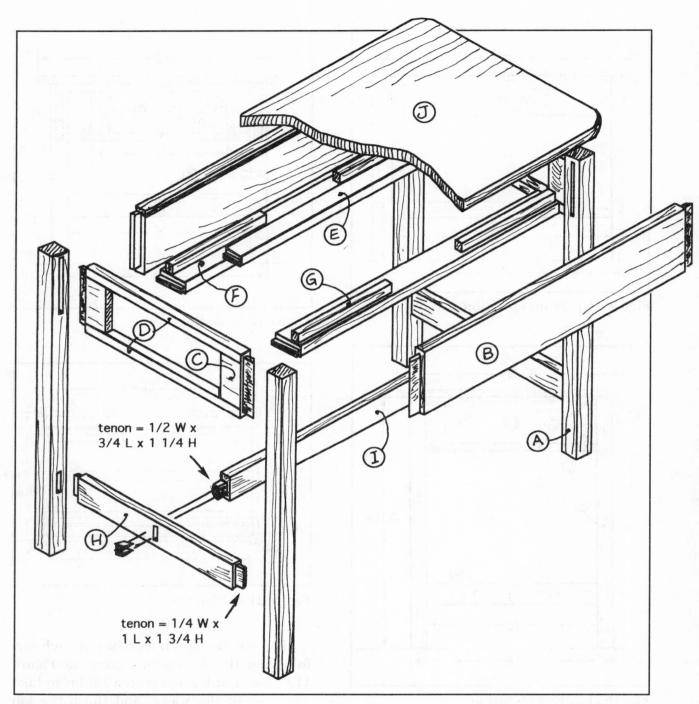

tenon = 1/2 W x
3/4 L x 1 1/4 H

tenon = 1/4 W x
1 L x 1 3/4 H

Figure 11.5. Exploded view

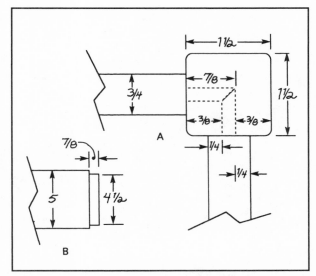

Figure 11.6. Leg and apron joinery details

the center. Now cut the miters on the ends of the tenons, which are $7/8''$ to the long point. Check the fit of each joint and adjust as necessary.

Lay out the mortises in the legs for the end stretchers. Center them in the legs and chop them $1/4''$ wide, $1 3/4''$ high, and $1 1/16''$ deep. Match the stretchers to the legs. Cut the tenons $1''$ long and check the fit.

Next cut mortises $1/2''$ wide by $1 1/4''$ high through the center of the stretchers. Now, working from the outside with a file or small chisel, widen the vertical dimension of the mortise by about $1/16''$, tapering it back to the inside dimension.

Cut the $1/4''$ mortises in the end aprons to receive the stub-tenoned drawer runners, Parts F. Use a $1/4''$ straight bit in the table-mounted router. Cut the mortises about $2 1/2''$ long to allow for side-to-side adjustment.

▪ **Note:** You can position the runners flush with the bottom rail, Part D. Alternatively, if you raise the runner about $1/16''$ above the rail, the drawer will not drag on it.

Rout a continuous groove $1/4''$ from the upper edge of the aprons. These grooves accommodate the kicker, Part E, and the cabinetmakers' buttons that secure the top.

Now cut the runners and kicker $26 1/4''$ long and make their $1/4''$ stub tenons in each end.

ASSEMBLING THE FRAME

Make a partial dry assembly to spot any potential problems and to determine the precise measurement for the center stretcher.

Clamp the legs to the end aprons and stretchers, then clamp those assemblies to the long aprons. Check that all joints are tight and square.

The distance between the side stretchers will be the shoulder-to-shoulder length of the center stretcher. The overall length of the stretcher should be about $1/4''$ longer than the outside-to-outside distance between the side stretchers. Cut the tenons to fit the inside dimensions of the mortises.

Cut two kerfs in each tenon to receive the wedges. Make the wedges out of hardwood.

Disassemble the desk. Round over the edges of the legs with a $1/4''$ bit and sand all the components.

Begin the final assembly with the ends. Apply glue to the apron and stretcher tenons, fit them into the legs, and clamp. Allow the ends to dry.

Place one end assembly flat on the bench. Apply glue to the tenons of the center stretcher, drawer runners, kicker, and long aprons, and slip them into their mortises. Bring the other side into place.

Upright the assembly, and clamp the ends together. Check the alignment of the drawer runners and kicker.

Finally, apply glue to the wedges, and tap them into the slots in the ends of the stretcher. When the glue has dried, trim off the excess and sand smooth.

MAKING AND FITTING THE DRAWERS

The measurements given for the drawer

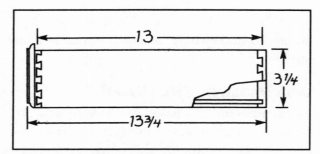

Figure 11.7. Drawer elevation

components allow for a ¼″ clearance top to bottom and side to side. The measurements also assume ¼″-long dovetails front and back. Adjust the measurements as necessary. Cut a ³⁄₈″ rabbet on the ends and top edges of the drawer fronts and round them over with a ¼″ bit before cutting the pins.

Sand the inside surfaces of the pieces before assembling the drawers. Sand the outsides thoroughly before fitting the drawers.

To fit the drawers, cut four guides, Parts G, ¾″ x ¾″ x 10″. Drill and countersink a pair of #6 pilot holes in each guide. Put the drawers in place and clamp the guides next to them. Test the drawers' action. When it's right, screw the guides to the runners with 1¼″ x 6 flathead screws. Don't glue the guides to the runners in case later adjustment is necessary.

FINISHING UP

Glue up the blank for the top. Work it smooth, then cut it 20″ wide by 30″ long. Round the corners with a 2″ radius. A decorative edge is optional.

Sand everything, then finish in the manner of your choosing.

Install the drawer pulls.

Use eight or so cabinetmakers' buttons (see Figure 9) with 1″ x 6 flathead screws to secure the top to the frame.

TYKE'S CHAIR

Designed to accompany Project 11, the tyke's chair is just right for preschoolers and early-graders. Its simple design and straight lines make it easy to build.

CONSIDERATIONS

Materials

Make the chair out of the same wood as the table. You will need about six board feet of lumber. The legs are $1\frac{1}{2}''$ square. Fashion them out of solid stock or laminate two pieces of $\frac{3}{4}''$ stock.

Special Tools and Cuts

The chair is held together entirely with pinned mortise and tenon joints. Use $\frac{3}{16}''$ dowel stock for the pins.

Treat the edges of all the pieces with a $\frac{1}{4}''$ round-over bit.

The seat is held to the frame with six $1\frac{1}{4}'' \times 8$ flathead screws driven through cleats with slotted pilot holes.

MAKING THE LEGS

Select the $1\frac{1}{2}''$ stock or laminate sufficient $\frac{3}{4}''$ stock for the legs. Cut the back legs, Parts A, 26" long, and the front legs, Parts B, $12\frac{1}{4}''$ long. Mark each leg according to its position in the chair.

Lay out the rails and their mortises. Each rail has a $\frac{1}{4}''$ rabbet cut on each edge, leaving a $\frac{1}{4}''$ tenon centered in its end.

Project 12 Material List

Item	Description	Quantity	Thickness	Width	Length	Comments
A	Back leg	2	1½″	1½″	26″	
B	Front leg	2	1½″	1½″	12¼″	
C	Back rail	2	¾″	2″	11″	1″ tenons
D	Back top rail	1	¾″	3″	11″	1″ tenons
E	Front rail	2	¾″	2″	12½″	1″ tenons
F	Side rail	4	¾″	2″	11″	1″ tenons
G	Cleat	2	¾″	1″	9¾″	
H	Seat	1	¾″	11″	14½″	
	Flathead screws	12	1¼″ x 8″			

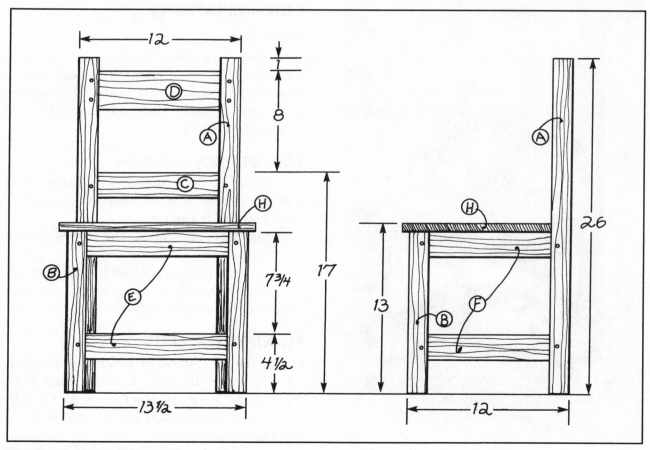

Figure 12.1. Front and side elevations

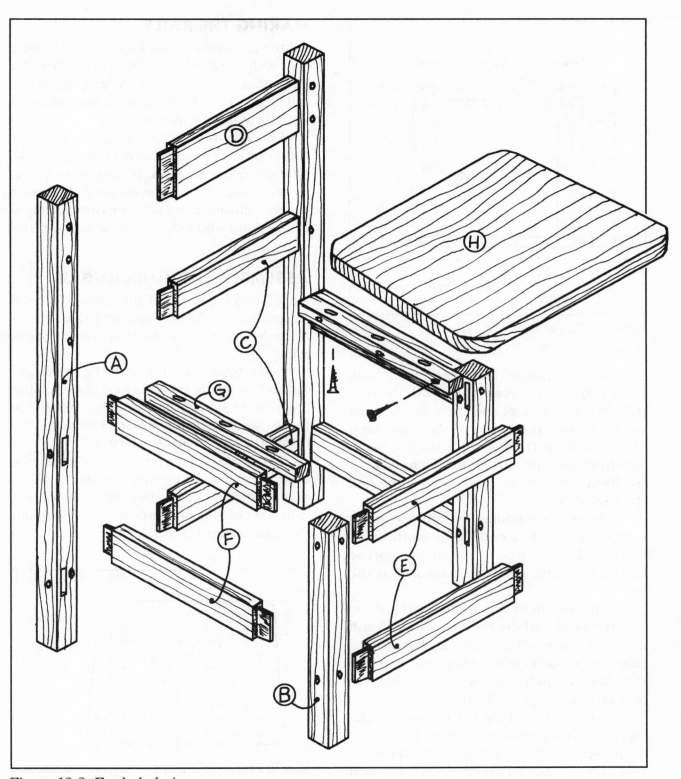

Figure 12.2. Exploded view

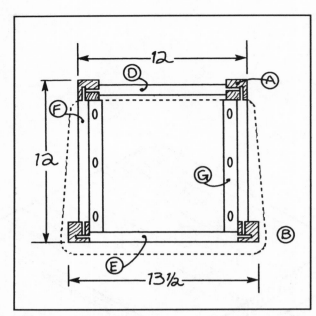

Figure 12.3. Section

Notice in Figure 12.3 that the outside faces of the side rails are flush with the outside of the back legs and their inside faces are flush with the inside of the front legs. This makes the front wider than the back. The front rails are flush with the outside of the front legs. The back rails are centered in the back legs.

Most of the rounding over of the edges must be done before cutting the mortises (so the pilot bearing won't drop into a mortise and ruin the cut) and before assembling the pieces.

It's important to stop routed cuts just before the points where the face of a rail will meet the face of a leg. Study the illustrations carefully to determine where to stop the cuts. You will finish the eventual inside corners after assembling the frame.

Be sure to round the bottom ends of the legs and the top ends of the back legs.

After rounding the edges, cut the mortises. Use a table-mounted router or a drill press.

MAKING THE RAILS

All the rails are 2″ wide except the top back rail, which is 3″. Cut the back and side rails, Parts C, D, and F, 11″ long and the front rails, Parts E, 12½″ long. Mark each rail end with its matching mortise.

Cut the tenons on a table-mounted router or a table saw. Cut each to fit its specific mortise; check the fit as you go along.

Next round over the edges of the rails. Do not, however, round over the top edges of the front and side rails that support the seat.

ASSEMBLY AND FINISHING UP

Make a dry assembly of the frame to check for problems. Check especially that everything is square and the rails are in alignment.

Begin final assembly with the back, gluing and clamping the rails into place. Clamp together the front-leg assembly. When the front- and back-leg assemblies are dry, clamp the side rails into place.

To pin the tenons, bore the ³⁄₁₆″ diameter holes all the way through the legs to allow excess glue to squeeze out the back. Wipe a thin layer of glue on the dowel, drive the pin through, and cut it flush.

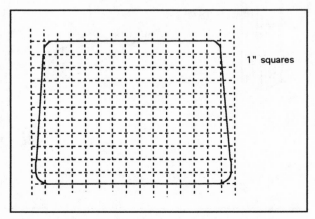

Figure 12.4. Seat pattern

Now turn your attention to the edges. Use a small chisel and sandpaper to finish the inside corners. Sand the entire frame thoroughly.

Glue and screw the cleats, Parts G, to the side rails. Bore three slotted pilot holes in each cleat.

Glue up stock for the seat with the grain running from side to side. After smoothing out the blank, cut the seat according to the pattern in Figure 12.4. Round over the edges with a ¼″ bit. Sand thoroughly.

Before you mount the seat with six 1¼″ x 8 flathead screws, apply the finish of your choice.

▪ Project 13 ▪
STUDY DESK

Once a child gets past third grade or so, homework more and more becomes a way of life. Every student needs a good place to study. Although I can't guarantee that the study desk presented here will make an "A" student, I can predict that, placed in a suitable environment, it will be a great place to do homework.

Project 13 Material List

Item	Description	Quantity	Thickness	Width	Length	Comments
A	Leg	4	$1\frac{1}{2}''$	$1\frac{1}{2}''$	$27\frac{1}{4}''$	
B1	Bottom rail	1	$\frac{3}{4}''$	$\frac{7}{8}''$	$38\frac{3}{4}''$	Parts for front apron, B1–5, are cut from a single piece of stock. See Figure 13.6.
B2	Top rail	1	$\frac{3}{4}''$	$\frac{3}{4}''$	$38\frac{3}{4}''$	
B3	Center spacer	1	$\frac{3}{4}''$	$4''$	$3''$	
B4	End spacer	2	$\frac{3}{4}''$	$4''$	$3\frac{7}{8}''$	
B5	Drawer front	2	$\frac{3}{4}''$	$3\frac{7}{8}''$	$13\frac{7}{8}''$	
C	Rear apron	1	$\frac{3}{4}''$	$5\frac{5}{8}''$	$38\frac{3}{4}''$	$\frac{7}{8}''$ tenon each end
D	Side apron	2	$\frac{3}{4}''$	$5\frac{5}{8}''$	$16\frac{3}{4}''$	$\frac{7}{8}''$ tenon each end
E	Drawer runner	4	$\frac{3}{4}''$	$2''$	$16\frac{1}{4}''$	stub tenon each end
F	Kicker	2	$\frac{3}{4}''$	$1\frac{1}{4}''$	$16\frac{1}{4}''$	stub tenon each end
G	Drawer guide	4	$\frac{3}{4}''$	$1''$	$8''$	
H	Side stretcher	2	$\frac{3}{4}''$	$2\frac{1}{4}''$	$17''$	$1''$ tenon each end
I	Center stretcher	1	$\frac{3}{4}''$	$2\frac{1}{4}''$	$39\frac{1}{4}''$	$\frac{3}{4}''$ tenon each end
J	Top	1	$\frac{3}{4}''$	$20''$	$42''$	
K	Drawer back	2	$\frac{1}{2}''$	$3\frac{7}{8}''$	$13\frac{7}{8}''$	
L	Drawer side	4	$\frac{1}{2}''$	$3\frac{7}{8}''$	$15''$	$\frac{1}{4}''$-long dovetails
M	Drawer bottom	2	$\frac{1}{4}''$	$13\frac{3}{8}''$	$15''$	A/C plywood
	Knob	2	$1\frac{3}{4}''$			diameter
	Flathead screws	10	$1'' \times 6''$			for cabinetmakers' buttons
	Flathead screws	8	$1\frac{1}{4}'' \times 6''$			for drawer guides
	Cabinetmakers' buttons	10				

CONSIDERATIONS

Materials

The desk pictured is made of solid pine. Because of the wood's softness, a desk mat is highly recommended. The drawers are flush mounted, with $\frac{3}{4}''$ fronts and $\frac{1}{2}''$ backs and sides. The drawer bottoms are made of $\frac{1}{4}''$ plywood. The project uses about twenty-four board feet of lumber, excluding the plywood.

Special Tools and Cuts

You will need these router bits:

$\frac{1}{4}''$ straight

$\frac{1}{4}''$ round-over

$\frac{1}{2}''$ round-over

$\frac{1}{2}''$ dovetail

The study desk uses mortise and tenon joinery. The tenons on the aprons are mitered to make use of their full length. The center stretcher is through-tenoned and wedged.

The front apron, which frames two drawers, shows an added touch of craftsmanship. It is cut apart to remove the drawer fronts and reassembled. When the drawers are in place, the grain pattern across the face of the apron will be maintained.

PREPARATIONS

Select the stock for the top and glue up the

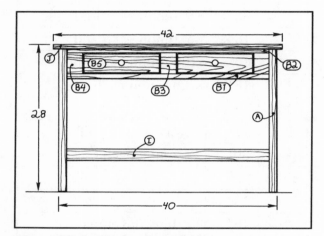

Figure 13.1. Front elevation

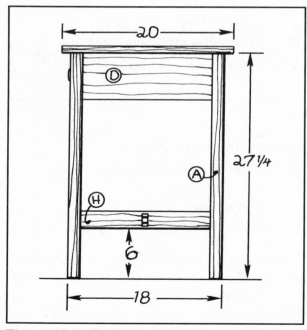

Figure 13.2. End elevation

blank. Work the joints flush and cut the blank to dimension. Use a ½" round-over bit, or other decorative bit, to edge the top. Do all four edges.

The legs are 1½" square. They can be cut from solid stock or laminated from ¾" stock.

Select the stock for the aprons, but don't rip it yet.

MAKING THE FRONT APRON

To make the front apron, begin with a piece of stock at least 40" long and at least 6" wide.

• **Note:** A 6" width is adequate if you use a sharp planer blade to rip the board. This will allow you to rejoin the pieces without further treatment. If you think you'll have to run the pieces over a jointer, begin with a wider board.

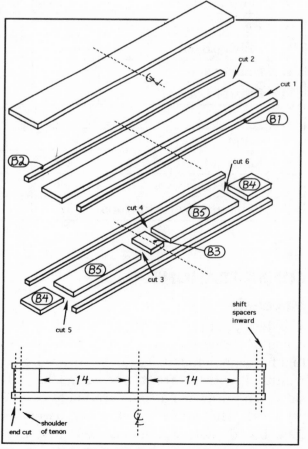

Figure 13.3. Front apron cutting scheme

Strike a line through the center of the board, as shown in Figure 13.3. Then mark the face of the board in such a way that will indicate the placement of the individual pieces once they're cut.

Rip the ⅞″ bottom rail, Part B1, first (or the ¾″ top rail—it doesn't matter as long as you work from one edge to the other). Set your saw at 4″ and rip the center piece, which will become the drawer fronts and spacers, Parts B3, B4, and B5. Do not yet rip the top rail, Part B2.

Working from the centerline, lay out and cut the center spacer, Part B3. Make sure you cut on the *outside* of the lines (away from the centerline).

Next cut the drawer fronts, Parts B5, 13⅞″ long, measuring from the edge closest to the center. What's left over are the end spacers, Parts B4.

Lay all the pieces on the bench in their correct position. Notice there is no top-to-bottom clearance for the drawer fronts. You will rip them to width later. You will also notice that the saw kerfs left way too much side-to-side clearance. Shift the end spacers toward the center until the openings are 14″ wide. Make new orientation marks for the relocated end spacers, then glue and clamp Parts B1, B2, B3, and B4 together.

MILLING THE PIECES

Now rip the aprons 5⅝″ wide. When ripping the front apron, remember to cut the waste off the *top* edge, leaving the top rail ¾″ wide. Cut the front and rear aprons, Parts B and C, 38¾″ long and the side aprons, Parts D, 16¾″ long.

Determine the position of the legs and mark them accordingly. Also mark the ends of each apron, matching them to the legs into which they will fit.

Lay out the apron mortises in each leg, using the dimensions given in Figure 13.4. Use a drill press with a ¼″ bit to take out

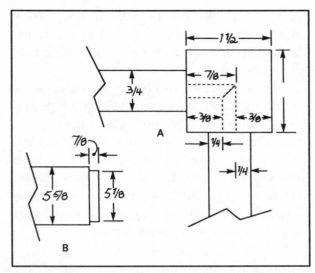

Figure 13.4. Leg and apron joinery details

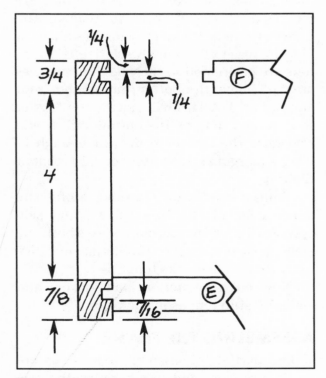

Figure 13.5. Apron section

most of the waste, and finish the job with a chisel. Or use a ¼″ straight bit in a table-mounted router.

Cut the tenons. The distance between the shoulders is 37″ for the front and rear aprons and 15″ for the side aprons. Now cut the miters on the ends of the tenons. Check the fit of each joint and adjust as necessary.

Lay out the mortises for the side stretchers. They are centered in the legs and are ¼″ wide and 1¾″ high. Chop them 1¹⁄₁₆″ deep. Cut the tenons 1″ long. Check the fit.

Now cut mortises ½″ wide by 1¼″ high through the center of the stretchers. Next, with a file or small chisel, widen the mortise vertically at the outside by about ¹⁄₁₆″. Taper the cuts to the inside dimension.

Chuck a ¼″ straight bit in the table-mounted router to cut the ¼″ mortises for the drawer runners and kickers as shown in Figure 13.5. The front and rear aprons are mortised at the bottom to receive the drawer runners. Make the mortises about 3″ long for ease of assembly. Notice the runners are positioned so their bearing surfaces are ¹⁄₁₆″ above the bottom rail of the front apron, Part B1. This will elevate the drawer so it doesn't drag on the bottom rail. It will also raise the drawer front just enough to leave a margin at the bottom equal to that at the top.

Rout a continuous groove along the upper edge of the front, back, and side aprons. This groove accommodates both the kickers, Parts F, and the cabinetmakers' buttons, which secure the top.

Now cut the runners and kickers and make ¼″ stub tenons in each end.

ASSEMBLING THE FRAME

Make a partial dry assembly to spot any potential problems and to determine the precise measurement for the center stretcher.

Clamp the legs to the side aprons and stretchers, then clamp those assemblies to the front and rear aprons. Check that all joints are tight and square.

The distance between the side stretchers will be the shoulder-to-shoulder length of

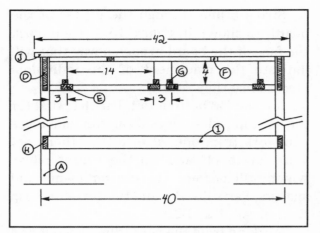

Figure 13.6. Section through sides

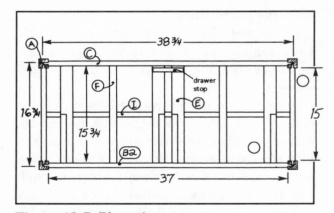

Figure 13.7. Plan view

the center stretcher. The overall length of the stretcher should be about ¼″ longer than the outside-to-outside distance between the side stretchers. Make the ½″ x 1¼″ tenons ⅞″ long.

Cut two kerfs in each tenon to receive the wedges. Make the wedges out of hardwood.

Disassemble the desk. Round over the legs with a ¼″ bit.

Begin the final assembly with the sides. Apply glue to the apron and stretcher tenons, fit them into the legs, and clamp. Allow the sides to dry.

Place one side flat on the bench. Apply glue to the tenons of the center stretcher

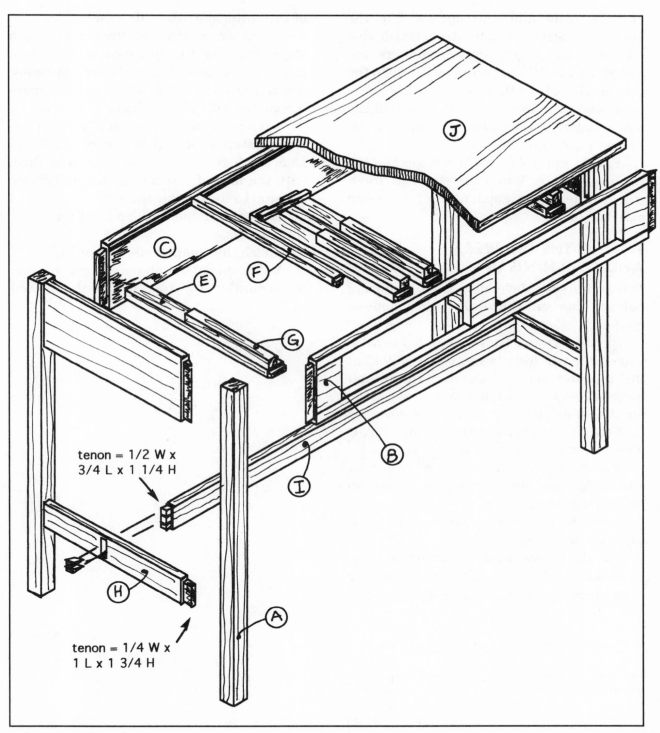

tenon = 1/2 W x
3/4 L x 1 1/4 H

tenon = 1/4 W x
1 L x 1 3/4 H

Figure 13.8. Exploded view

and the front and rear aprons. Slip the aprons and stretcher into place. Brush glue on the tenons of the drawer runners and kickers and put them into place between the aprons. Bring the other side into place.

Upright the assembly and clamp all the pieces together. Check the alignment of the drawer runners and kickers.

Finally, apply glue to the wedges and tap them into place. When the glue has dried, trim off the excess length of the tenons and sand smooth.

FITTING THE DRAWERS AND FINISHING UP

The drawers are dovetailed front and back, but you can substitute any other suitable method.

Rip the fronts, sides, and backs 3⅞" wide. This will leave a clearance of ¹⁄₁₆" at the top and bottom. Cut the fronts and backs 13⅞" long. The measurements given for the sides and bottom assume dovetails ¼" long. The drawer bottoms are of ¼" A/C plywood let into ¼"-deep grooves.

Round over the top edges of the sides and back. Sand the inside surfaces before assembling the drawers.

Sand the outsides of the drawers, then slip them into their openings.

Cut the drawer guides, Parts G, 8" long. Drill two pilot holes in each. Place a drawer in its opening, making it flush with the face

of the apron and even side to side. Place the drawer guides next to the drawer, leaving a slight clearance. Clamp the guides into place and slide the drawers in and out a few times. When you're satisfied with the fit, secure the guides with 1¼" x 6 flathead screws.

Cut a piece of scrap about 5" long for the drawer stop as shown in Figures 13.7 and 13.8. With the drawers in place and flush with the face of the apron, glue and clamp the stop to the drawer runners.

Sand the frame, top, and drawer fronts thoroughly.

Finish the components as you like.

Make ten or so cabinetmakers' buttons for mounting the top. Install the drawer pulls.

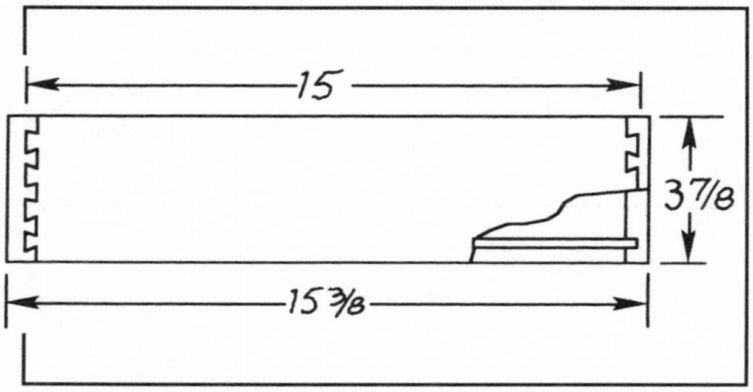

Figure 13.9. Drawer elevation

▪ Project 14 ▪
COMPUTER STATION

Many students become interested in computers at an early age. By the time they begin high school, a computer is an integral part of their study routine. A desk with a computer on it is no longer a desk, but a station.

The computer station includes ample space on the desktop for a computer and monitor; a pull-out keyboard tray neatly hidden behind a false drawer front; a concealed printer and paper carriage, which slides out for easy access; and built-in storage for floppy disks. It also features a hutch with one fixed and one adjustable shelf.

Inherent with the use of computers is an unsightly tangle of wires and cables. It's inevitable that the standard two-outlet receptacle will need enhancing with a power strip. That doesn't mean, however, that the power strip and all the wires have to lie on the floor under the desk. There is plenty of room inside the printer cabinet to mount a power strip. This allows you to keep most of the wires and cables out of sight.

Project 14 Material List

Item	Description	Quantity	Thickness	Width	Length	Comments
A	Leg stile	6	3/4"	2"	29 1/4"	
B	Center stile	3	3/4"	2"	23 3/4"	
C	Rail	6	3/4"	2"	18"	
D	Panel	6	1/4"	8 1/4"	23 3/4"	A3 plywood
E	Frame rail/front	1	3/4"	2"	45 1/2"	
F	Frame rail/rear	1	3/4"	1 3/4"	45"	
G	Frame end/center	3	3/4"	1 1/4"	18"	
H	Rail	3	3/4"	2"	22 3/8"	
I	Bottom	1	3/4"	22 3/8"	19 1/4"	fir or oak plywood
J	Shelf	1	3/4"	11 1/2"	22 3/8"	
K	Bracket	2	3/4"	4"	5"	
L	Back	1	1/4"	26 1/4"	45 1/4"	A3 cut to configure
M	Top	1	3/4"	22 1/2"	48"	
N	Door stile	2	3/4"	2"	19 1/4"	no clearance
O	Door rail	2	3/4"	2"	17 7/8"	no clearance
P	Door panel	1	1/4"	18 3/8"	15 3/4"	A3 plywood
Q	Applied front	2	3/4"	4 7/8"	21 3/4"	1/16" clearance
R	Drawer front/back	2	1/2"	4"	21 5/8"	
S	Drawer side	2	1/2"	4"	19"	
T	Drawer bottom	1	1/4"	21 1/8"	19"	
U	Drawer partition	1	1/2"	4 1/8"	21 1/8"	
V	Partition	3	1/4"	3 3/4"	3 1/2"	
W	Carriage top/ bottom	2	3/4"	18"	12"	plywood or solid
X	Carriage posts	4			4 1/4"	1" dia. dowels

(Material list continued next page)

Item	Description	Quantity	Thickness	Width	Length	Comments
Y	Spacer	2	$1\frac{1}{2}''$	1″	12″	or as needed
Z	Keyboard tray	1	$\frac{3}{4}''$	$18\frac{7}{8}''$	12″	w/lip on back edge
AA	Side	2	$\frac{3}{4}''$	$7\frac{1}{2}''$	25″	
BB	Shelf	1	$\frac{3}{4}''$	$7\frac{1}{2}''$	45″	
CC	Partition	1	$\frac{3}{4}''$	$7\frac{1}{4}''$	$21\frac{1}{2}''$	
DD	Top rail	1	$\frac{3}{4}''$	3″	45″	
EE	Bottom rail	1	$\frac{3}{4}''$	4″	$45\frac{1}{4}''$	
FF	Back	1	$\frac{1}{4}''$	18″	$45\frac{1}{4}''$	A3 plywood
GG	Shelf	1	$\frac{3}{4}''$	$7\frac{1}{4}''$	$21\frac{3}{4}''$	
	Center-mount slide	3		19″		
	Drawer/door pull	3		$\frac{7}{16}''$ dia.		wire-type
	Magnetic catch	2				
	Brass chain	1		6″		approximate length
	No-mortise hinge	1		pr.		for keyboard tray front
	Hinge	1		pr.		butt or butterfly type
	Shelf pins	4				brass or other
	Flathead screws	2		1″ x 8″		for applied drawer front
	Flathead screws			$1\frac{1}{4}''$ x 8″		to secure top
	Flathead screws	14		2″ x 8″		for hutch and printer carriage

CONSIDERATIONS

Materials

This computer station is made of oak. The door and the three leg assemblies are of frame-and-panel construction, with ¼″ A3 plywood for the panels. The case and hutch backs are also oak plywood. The bottom, which supports the printer carriage, is ¾″ A/C fir plywood, but any suitable stock will do. The drawer bottom is ¼″ A/C fir plywood.

The project will use about forty-three board feet of solid oak and one 4′ x 8′ sheet of A3 oak plywood.

• **Note:** Much imported ¼″ hardwood plywood is less than its nominal thickness. Adjust the grooves and stub tenons accordingly.

The computer station uses several pieces of hardware that may not be available locally. They are readily available by mail order, however.

For the keyboard tray, you will need a 12″ Accuride Series 2008 slide set. This slide locks in the extended position.

The drawer uses a 19″ center-mount Accuride Series 1029 slide.

The printer carriage uses a pair of 19″ Accuride Series 1029 slides to support the added weight of the printer. A slide of shorter length can be substituted, but one

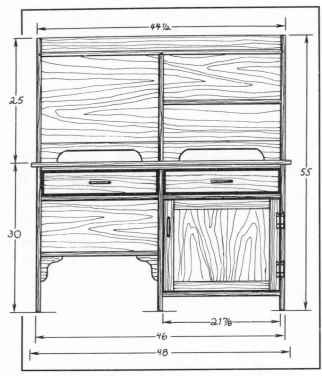

Figure 14.1. Front elevation

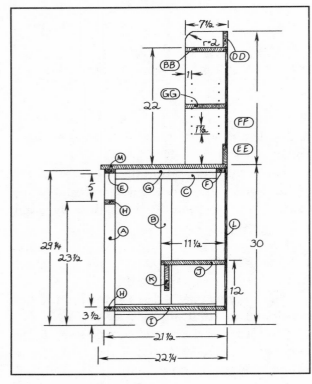

Figure 14.2. Section

19″ long allows the printer carriage to come fully out of the cabinet.

The false front that hides the keyboard tray swings down on an unobtrusive no-mortise hinge with a flat-black finish. A short length of brass chain holds the front when open, and a magnetic catch secures it when closed.

The door to the printer cabinet swings on a pair of butterfly hinges and is held shut with a magnetic catch.

The door and drawer pulls are $7/16$″ diameter oak wire-type.

The adjustable shelf rests on four $1/4$″ brass pins.

Special Tools and Cuts

You will need these router bits:

$3/16$″ cove
$1/4$″ straight
$1/4$″ round-over
$1/2$″ round-over
$1/2$″ dovetail
$3/4$″ straight

Stub tenons and sliding dovetails make up most of the joints in the computer station. The drawers are joined with $1/2$″ dovetails. The top is rounded over and filleted with a $1/2$″ bit.

CONSTRUCTING THE CASE

Glue Up Top

Select the pieces to make the top and true up their edges. Glue and clamp the pieces together.

Work the surfaces smooth and rip and cut the blank to size. Use a $1/2$″ round-over or other decorative bit to treat the front and side edges.

Build Leg Panels

Rip the frame members of the leg panels 2″ wide. While you're at it, rip the 2″ stock needed for the case and the door. Cut all the pieces to rough length.

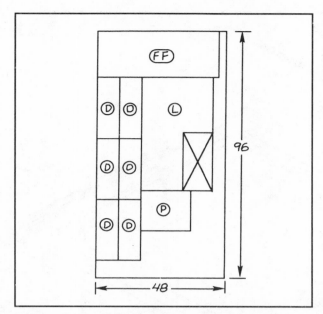

Figure 14.3. Plywood cutting scheme

Lay all the pieces on the bench as they will be in the panels and mark the outside faces and the edges to be grooved.

The fastest way to groove the rails and stiles is by making two passes on a table saw, one with each face against the fence. This automatically centers the groove. It also allows for a fine adjustment of the width of the groove to match the thickness of the plywood. Remember to groove the door members now so you won't have to reset your saw later.

▪ **Note:** The lengths given for the rails and stiles in the door reflect the inside dimensions of the frame of the printer cabinet. You may wish to assemble the door now and trim it to fit later. Or wait to assemble the door after the case is assembled and you can take the exact measurements of the opening.

Although the finished leg panels are 29¼″ tall, cut the leg stiles, Parts A, about ⅛″ longer. The excess will be trimmed later. This eliminates the need to match precisely the upper edge of the top rail with the top ends of the legs.

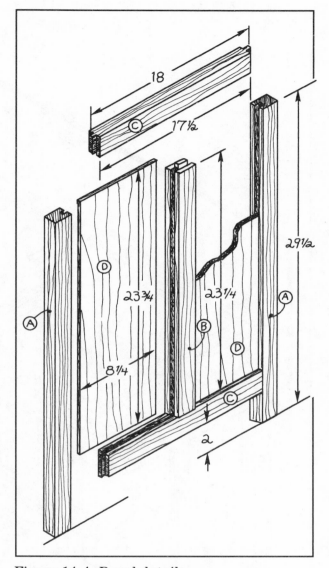

Figure 14.4. Panel details

Cut the center stiles, Parts B, and the rails, Parts C, to length. Remember to allow for the tenons on each end. Cut the plywood panels in sets to maintain grain continuity in the finished panels. Refer to Figure 14.3 for an oak plywood cutting scheme.

Mark the positions of the center stiles on the rails and the rails on the legs.

Brush a little glue into the grooves to hold the panels in place. Begin the assembly by gluing the center stile into position in the

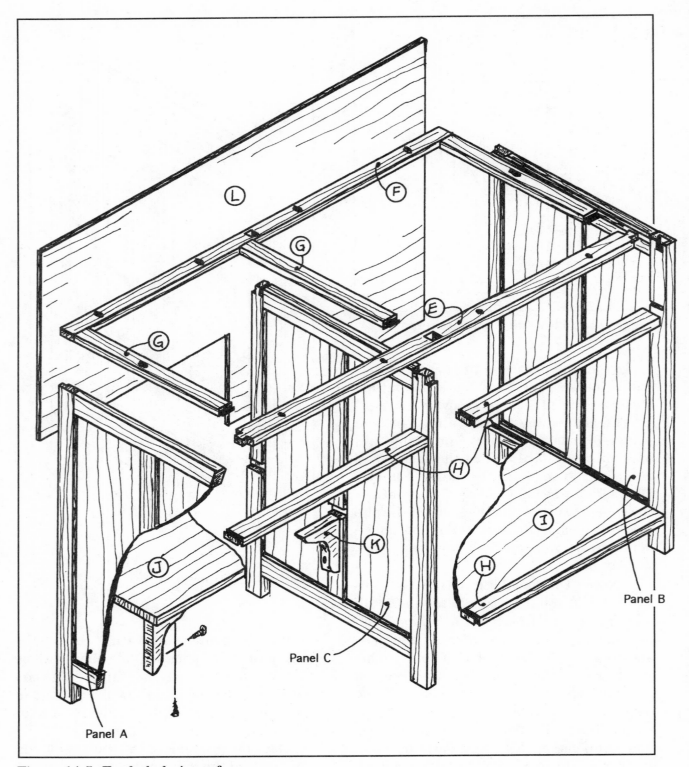

Figure 14.5. Exploded view of case

bottom rail. Bring the plywood panels into place and fit the top rail. Now fit the leg stiles. Clamp the pieces together, making sure all the pieces are properly located and the assembly is square. When dry, trim the top of the legs flush with the rail.

Determine the position of the panels within the case and mark them A, B, or C as shown in Figure 14.5. Using a ¾″ straight bit, cut the ¼″-deep rabbets in panels A and B. Also cut the ¼″ dadoes in the bottom rails of panels B and C. The rabbets and dadoes must be stopped 2″ from the front edge of the panels. Next cut the ¼″-deep dadoes in the stiles of panels A and C to accept the shelf, Part J.

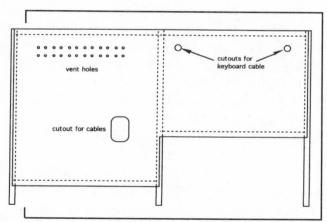

Figure 14.6. Back view showing rabbet cuts and cable cutouts

Cut a ¼″ x ⅜″ rabbet in the back edges of panels A and B for the back, Part L. The rabbets need only run down the edges as far as the shelf dado in panel A and the bottom dado in panel B as shown in Figure 14.6. Panel C requires a different treatment. Remove ¼″ of the back edge down to the bottom of the dado for the shelf, Part J. The cut continues as a ⅜″ rabbet through the dado for the bottom, Part I.

Now fit your router with the ½″ dovetail bit set at ¼″. Cut the dovetailed slots for the

rails, Parts H. Take care in laying out and cutting the slots to ensure correct alignment of the rails. Stop each slot ¼″ from the edge of the panel.

Mill and Assemble Framing

Cut the rails, Parts H, to length, and set up to cut the dovetailed tenons. Make several test cuts to ensure a snug fit.

Mark the ends of each rail to correspond to their positions in the panels (A, B, C) and cut the dovetailed tenons. Trim the front edges of the tenons to fit the stop. *Without* glue, assemble the rails and panels.

Now cut the front rail, Part E, to length and cut the dovetailed tenons on each

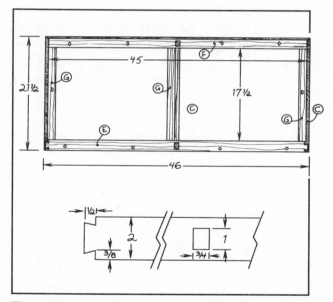

Figure 14.7. Plan view of top frame and dovetailed tenons of Rail E

end. Make certain the shoulder-to-shoulder length of the rail matches the inside-to-inside measurement between panels A and B. Locate the center of the rail and chop the ¾″ x 1″ mortise.

Lay the rail in place across the panels. Mark the mortises for the dovetails in panels A and B and the tenon in panel C.

Cut the rear frame rail, Part F, to length. Notice that it is 1/4" narrower and 1/2" shorter than the front rail. Locate and cut the 3/4" x 3/4" mortise in the center of the rail.

Disassemble the rails and panels. Chop the dovetailed mortises in panels A and B and cut the tenons in panel C. Check the fit of each joint.

Lay out and cut the mortises for the center and end rails, Parts G, in the front and rear frame rails. Then cut the stub tenons in the rails.

Cut Brackets and Shelves

Refer to Figure 14.8 for the bracket pattern. Make two brackets, then bore and counterbore holes for 1 1/2" x 8 flathead screws.

▪ **Note:** The length of screw will depend on the depth of the counterbore. Make sure the screws you use will not pierce the shelf or the stiles.

Cut the shelf, Part J, and the bottom, Part I.

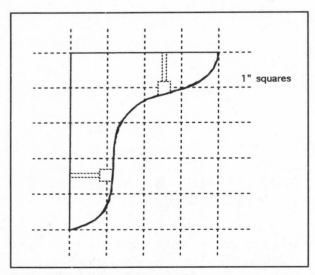

1" squares

Figure 14.8. Bracket detail

Assemble Case

Make another dry assembly of the case to ensure that all the pieces fit as expected. In addition, it's easier to glue individual pieces

into the assembly when most of the components are clamped together.

Begin with the rails, Parts H, then fit the front rail, Part E. Slip Parts G into their mortises in the front rail, and complete the frame with the rear rail, Part F. Run a bar clamp across the rear rail to hold the end panels tight to the frame.

Slide the bottom, Part I, into its dadoes and clamp panels B and C across the back edge of the bottom to secure the pieces.

Do the same for the shelf, Part J, adding a clamp across the bottom of the panels at the center if necessary.

Mark the positions of the center and end rails, Parts G, and remove the top frame pieces. Now glue and clamp the top frame together, making certain it is square.

Remove the shelf and the bottom from the assembly, and tap out the rail that faces the bottom. Apply glue to the tenons, and replace the rail. Brush glue into the dadoes for the bottom and along the bottom's leading edge. Slide the bottom into place, and clamp it front to back and side to side.

Glue in the drawer rail.

Apply glue to the dovetailed mortises and rabbets in panels A and B, and the tenons in panel C. Tap the top frame into place and clamp.

Remove the keyboard tray rail. Brush glue into the shelf dadoes in the stiles of panels A and C. Spread the panels apart just enough to bring the shelf into place. Bring the panels back together, and clamp them against the shelf. Apply glue to the brackets, and screw them into place.

Glue the keyboard tray rail into its slots.

Turn the case onto its face. Check for square across the back. Apply glue to the edges of the panels and shelves, and tack down the back, Part L.

CONSTRUCTING THE HUTCH

Sliding dovetails and rabbet joints are used to join the hutch. Begin by ripping the

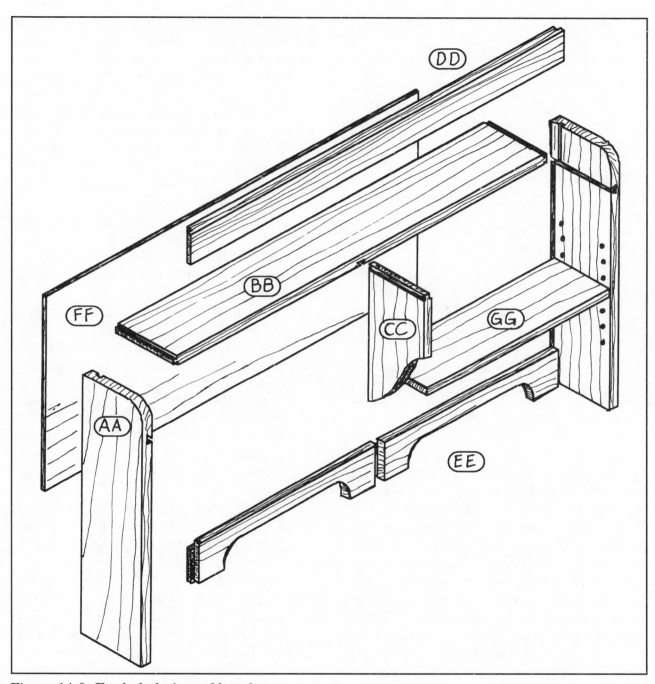

Figure 14.9. Exploded view of hutch

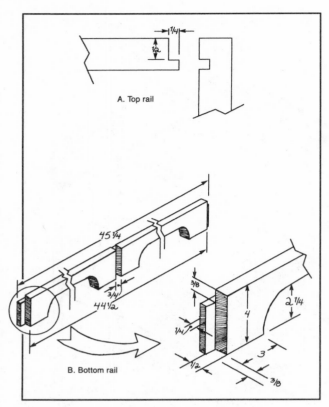

Figure 14.10. Hutch rail details

measured to the shoulder cut. Be sure to add the length of the dovetail. Cut the sliding dovetail on the partition's top end.

Cut a ¼" by ⅜" rabbet up the back edge of each side, stopping it at the dovetail slot. Cut the same size rabbet on the bottom rear edge of the shelf. Then cut a ¼" x ¼" dado in the sides for the top rail, Part DD, as shown in Figure 14.10A. Stop the cut at the dovetail slot. Cut corresponding rabbets in the ends of the top rail.

Cut the bottom rail, Part EE, to length, then cut the ⅜" x ½" rabbets in each end (Figure 14.10B). Make sure the shoulder-to-shoulder length of the rail matches that of the shelf.

Next cut a ¼" x ⅜" rabbet along the rail's upper back edge.

Now lay out the cutouts and the dado at the center. Make the cutouts first and sand them smooth. Use a ¼" round-over bit to round over the forward top edge of the rail and inside edges of the cutouts. Finally, cut the ¾"-wide by ½"-deep dado in the center of the rail.

Cut the 2" radius arcs in the upper corners of the sides.

The last thing to do before final assembly of the hutch is to bore the holes for the adjustable-shelf pins, as shown in Figure 14.2.

▪ **Note:** Pins come in different diameters. Have on hand the pins you will use before you bore the holes.

Begin the assembly by brushing glue on one of the dovetailed tenons of the shelf. Insert the tenon into the slot from the back, thus forcing the squeeze-out to the back. Next, brush glue into the slot of the remaining side. Slide it into place from the back. Brush glue onto the partition tenon and slip it into place. After bringing each piece into position, check that their leading edges are flush.

Apply glue to the ends and bottom edge

pieces to the widths given in the material list. Cut the sides, Parts AA, and the shelf, Part BB, to length. Cut the partition, Part CC, ½" or so longer than specified. Lay out the slots in the sides and in the center of the shelf. Use a ½" dovetail bit and cut the slots ¼" deep. Back up the cuts to avoid tear-out.

Next set up to cut the dovetails in the ends of the shelf and the partition. Use a test piece the same width as the shelf. The fit should be looser than that of the rails in the case. The pieces should slide together, but without being sloppy. If the fit is too tight without glue, chances are that *with* glue the pieces will seize before they are in place.

Make a dry assembly of the shelf and at least one of the sides. Measure the distance from the bottom of the shelf to the bottom of the side. This is the length of the partition of the top rail. Slip it into place, and clamp it across the back and against the shelf.

Again check the joints at the front. If necessary, run a clamp across the front of the shelf.

With the assembly on its face, glue and clamp the bottom rail into place.

Check the assembly for square. Glue and tack the back into position.

CONSTRUCTING THE ACCESSORIES
Keyboard Tray

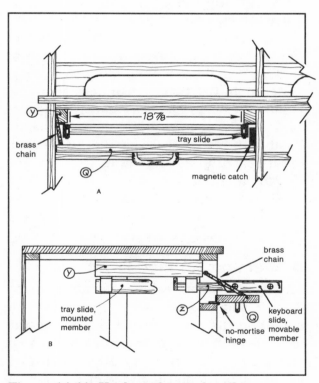

Figure 14.11. Keyboard tray details

The keyboard tray is 12″ wide and 18⅞″ long. The width includes a lip on the back edge (Figure 14.11) to prevent the keyboard from inadvertently slipping off. You can glue up the keyboard tray, Part Z, from solid stock, but it's a good place to use a scrap of oak plywood. If you use plywood, face the front edge with a strip of solid stock.

Printer Carriage

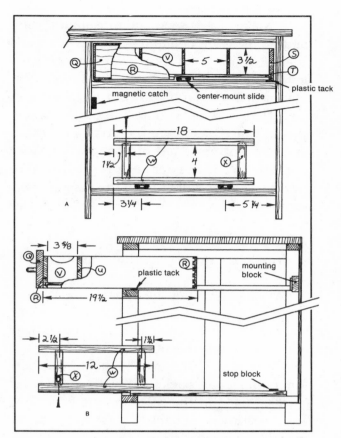

Figure 14.12. Drawer and printer stand details

The printer carriage is made from two pieces of stock 12″ wide by 18″ long separated by four 1″ diameter dowels. Again, plywood is a good substitute for solid stock.

The dowels are 4¼″ long and set into holes ⅛″ deep. Lay out and bore the holes according to the diagrams in Figure 14.12.

• **Note:** Sand and finish the printer carriage components before assembling with eight countersunk 2″ x 8 flathead screws. Drill pilot holes first to avoid splitting the dowels.

Drawer
The drawer front, back, and sides are ½″

thick and 4″ wide. Their lengths are calculated for dovetail joints, but other methods can be substituted.

▪ **Note:** The use of center-mount slide makes its own demands on the drawer's specifications. First, the drawer must have a length that corresponds with one of several mounting holes on the drawer member. Second, to ensure optimum slide performance, the distance between the drawer bottom and the bottom edge of the drawer sides must be ¼″. If the distance is greater than ¼″, the drawer will drag on the plastic tacks supplied with the slide (Figure 14.12). If the distance is less than ¼″, the drawer will wobble.

The long drawer partition, Part U, is 3½″ wide.

After machining the dovetails and pins, use a ¼″ bit to round over the top edges of the sides and the long partition. Round over only the inside edge of the drawer front.

Cut a ¼″ x ¼″ groove for the drawer bottom in the front, back, and sides. Then cut a ¼″ x ½″ dado in the sides for the partition. The partition is set back 3⅝″ from the inside face of the drawer front.

Next lay out and cut the ¼″ x ¼″ dadoes for the intermediate partitions, Parts V. Cut the partitions themselves from ¼″ plywood (or thinner if available). The cutouts at the top of the partitions are optional.

Assemble the drawer, but *do not* glue the partitions into place.

Door and Applied Fronts

Assemble the door, allowing for 1/16″ clearance on all sides. Cut the stiles about ¼″ long to leave ⅛″ ears on each end. Trim them after the glue has set. Cut a slight bevel on the catch side of the door.

Rip the applied fronts from a single piece of stock to maintain the grain pattern. Cut a 3/16″ cove around the perimeter of each piece. This optional cut adds visual interest

to the drawers and makes fitting the fronts much easier.

FINAL ASSEMBLY

Thoroughly sand and finish all the components before final assembly.

Keyboard Tray and False Front

Glue spacers, Parts Y, to the underside of the end rail and center rail (Figure 14.11). Mount the spacers about 1⅜″ in from the face of the case to allow clearance for the false front and its chain stop.

Mount the slides according to the provided directions.

Use a pair of no-mortise hinges to mount the applied front. Take care to get the front centered in the opening. Mount the magnetic catch. Use two ⅝″ pan-head screws to mount the brass chain as shown in Figure 14.11. In the open position, the front should be able to rest at least parallel to the rail, but it may drop slightly lower.

Mount the drawer pull.

Drill one or two 1″ diameter holes in the back of the cabinet to accommodate the keyboard cable (See Figure 14.6).

Drawer and Applied Front

The fixed portion (cabinet member) of the drawer slide comes with an adapter for mounting the rear end of the slide to the back of the cabinet (in the absence of a rear frame rail). Glue and screw from the back a mounting block on the inside of the cabinet as shown in Figure 14.12B. Follow the mounting instructions that come with the slide.

▪ **Note:** Depending on your method of drawer construction, you may need to notch the drawer back to accommodate the slide.

Tap the plastic tacks into place on each end of the rail. Be sure they are back far enough that they will not interfere with the applied front.

Insert the drawer. Check its alignment with the face of the case and its side-to-side position in the opening. Make any necessary adjustments by moving the fixed portion of the slide.

• **Hint:** The importance of correct clearance between the drawer bottom and the bottom edge of the sides has been commented on earlier. If the drawer drags, shim the fixed member of the slide until the drawer glides evenly on the plastic tacks. If the clearance is right and the drawer still wobbles, it's likely that there is a ''belly'' in the drawer bottom, which effectively decreases the clearance. You will need to rout (with a table-mounted ³/₄″ straight bit) or scrape a channel in the drawer bottom to make a level bed for the slide.

With the drawer in place, tightly shim the applied front in the opening. Drive two 1″ x 8 flathead screws through the inside of the drawer front into the applied front.

To install the drawer pull with the supplied screws, you will have to counterbore the holes into the drawer front from the inside.

If necessary, glue a stop to the mounting block at the back of the cabinet.

Printer Carriage and Door

Mount the fixed portions of the two printer carriage slides ⁷/₈″ in from the face of the cabinet. Mount the sliding portions as shown in Figure 14.12, and insert the carriage. Run the carriage into the cabinet until it's ⁷/₈″ from the face. Mount a stop on the cabinet bottom.

Shim the door into place and install the hinges. Check the swing, and mount the pull and the magnetic catch.

Cut a 2¹/₂″ x 4″ hole (or larger if necessary) in the cabinet back in a position that will accommodate a power strip and its cord without interfering with the drawer or carriage. Bore a series of ³/₁₆″ vent holes (Figure

14.6). Mount the power strip to the cabinet back.

Top and Hutch

Remove the drawer and printer carriage.

Drill a series of holes around the perimeter of the top frame (Figure 14.5). Make slotted holes on the side and back rails to allow for expansion and contraction of the top.

Place the top on the case and the hutch on the top. Center the hutch between the top's sides and flush with the back edge. Lightly mark the footprint of the hutch sides and partition. Remove the hutch. Bore two holes within each footprint, approximately ³/₄″ in from the front and back. (Shift the top so you don't damage the case.)

Replace the hutch and drive two 2″ x 8 flathead screws upward through the top into each of the hutch sides and the partition. You may need someone to hold the hutch in place during the operation. Make sure the screws are adequately countersunk so the heads don't drag on the top frame.

Center the hutch–top assembly on the case. Secure the top with 1¹/₄″ x 8 flathead screws.

Reinstall the drawer and printer carriage.

▪ Project 15 ▪

VANITY

The vanity features a large mirror, a pair of accent trays with small drawers, and a large center drawer below the top.

CONSIDERATIONS

Materials

Oak or another hardwood is a good choice for the vanity. You will need about thirty board feet, excluding the plywood for the drawer bottoms and mirror backer board.

The front of the main drawer is made from 3/4" stock. The sides and back are 1/2" thick and can be made of pine or other less expensive wood.

The accent trays, as well as the small drawer fronts and backs, are made of 1/2" stock. The drawer sides are 1/4".

The main drawer has a bail-type brass pull. The accent drawers have small brass knobs.

Special Tools and Cuts

You will need:

> 1/4" straight bit
> 1/4" round-over bit
> 3/8" rabbet bit with pilot
> 1/2" round-over bit
> 1/2" dovetail bit
> tapering jig

The legs are tapered on the inside faces, adding to the vanity's elegance. Tapering jigs are commercially available and easy to use. You can also make one from a piece of plywood, as shown in Figure 15.8. Cut the desired taper on one edge of the plywood. Tack a stop on the wide end. Place the leg against the stop, and run the jig along the fence of your table saw.

▪ **Caution:** Use appropriate hold-downs and push sticks while you cut the tapers. Work safely.

Project 15 Material List

Item	Description	Quantity	Thickness	Width	Length	Comments
A	Leg	4	1½"	1½"	27¼"	taper to 1" square
B	Rail	2	¾"	1¼"	33"	dovetail ends
C	Spacer	2	¾"	4"	6¾"	
D	Back apron	1	¾"	5½"	33"	
E	Side apron	2	¾"	5½"	18"	
F	Drawer runner	2	¾"	2"	16"	
G	Kicker	1	¾"	1¼"	16"	
H	Drawer guide	2	¾"	¾"	12"	
I	Top	1	¾"	20"	36"	cut out at front
J	Drawer front	1	¾"	3⅞"	18⅜"	
K	Drawer back	1	½"	3⅞"	18⅜"	
L	Drawer side	2	½"	3⅞"	15"	assumes ¼" tails
M	Drawer bottom	1	¼"	15"	17⅞"	plywood
N	Mirror rail	2	¾"	1½"	16"	stub tenon each end
O	Mirror stile	2	¾"	1½"	24"	
P	Backer board	1	¼"	16¼"	21¾"	
Q	Bracket	2	¾"	1¼"	24"	
R	Tray side	4	½"	5½"	6"	
S	Tray back	2	½"	6"	7¼"	
T	Tray shelf	4	½"	5½"	7¼"	
U	Drawer front/back	4	½"	2¹¹⁄₁₆"	6¹¹⁄₁₆"	
V	Drawer side	4	¼"	2¹¹⁄₁₆"	5"	assumes ¼" tails
W	Drawer bottom	2	¼"	4¾"	6⁷⁄₁₆"	plywood
	Cabinetmakers' buttons					
	Flathead screws		1" x 6"			
	Flathead screws	6	1¼" x 6"			for mirror bracket
	Flathead screws		1¼" x 8"			
	Drawer pull	1				bail-type
	Drawer pull	2				knob
	Mirror	1	16⅛" x 21⅝"			plate glass

Notice the cutout at the front edge of the top (Figure 15.3). Accommodate the cutout by moving the front apron inward, anchoring it to the side aprons with dovetailed tenons. The back and side aprons are fixed to the legs with mortise and tenon joints pinned with 3/16″ diameter dowels.

Use stub tenons to join the mirror frame.

Join the drawers with ½″ dovetails and the accent trays with ½″ sliding dovetails.

CONSTRUCTING THE TABLE
Glue Up Top

Select the stock for the top and glue it up. Make the blank an inch or so longer and wider than needed. Smooth out the blank and set it aside.

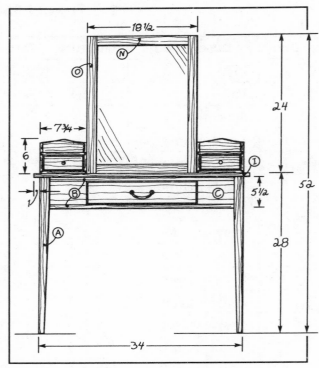

Figure 15.1. Front elevation

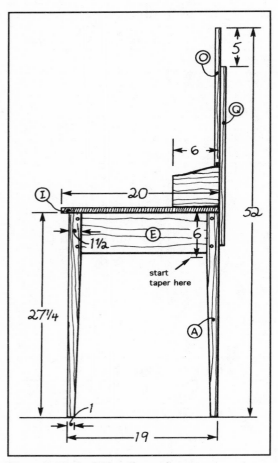

Figure 15.2. Side elevation

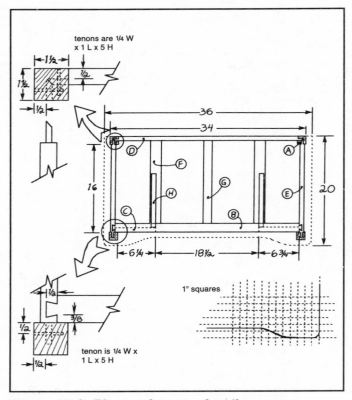

Figure 15.3. Plan and tenon details

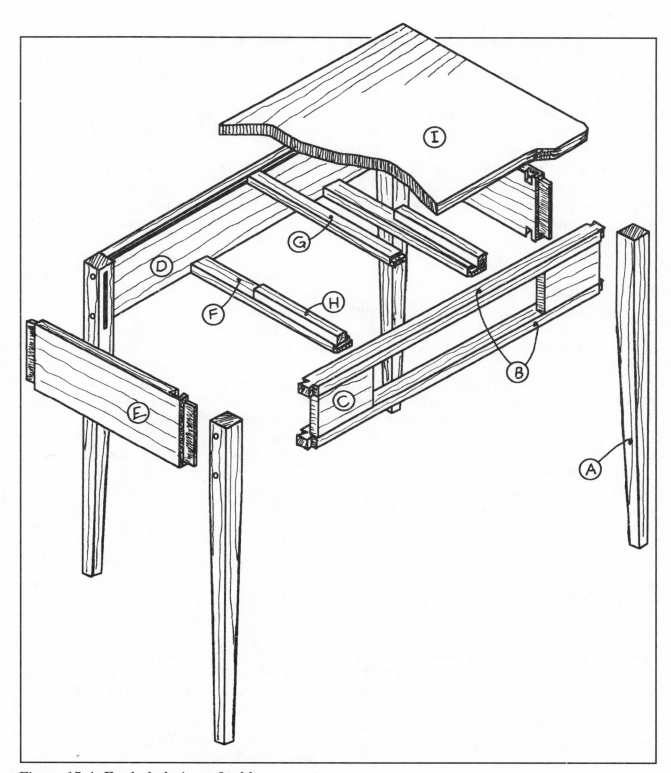

Figure 15.4. Exploded view of table

Mortise and Taper Legs

Cut the legs 27½″ long. Mark each leg according to its position in the table. Lay out the aprons and their mortises and the tapers on the legs.

Make the mortises ¼″ wide and 5″ high. Notice in Figure 15.3 that the mortises are *not* centered in the legs. Rather, they are located ½″ in from the outside face of the legs. Notice also how this, along with the position of the tenons in the back apron, allows the back apron to be flush with the back legs while maintaining the symmetry of the mortises.

Taper the legs, then chop the mortises 1″ deep.

Make Aprons and Rails

Rip the back apron, Part D, and the side aprons, Parts E, 5½″ wide. Cut the side aprons 21″ long and the back apron 33″ long.

Center the tenons in the side aprons with ¼″ rabbet cuts on both the inside and outside faces. The tenons on the back apron, however, are formed with a single ½″ rabbet cut on the outside face. Miter the tenons as shown in Figure 15.3.

The front apron is composed of two rails and two spacers. Both rails fit into dovetailed mortises cut in the upper and lower edges of the side aprons. Rip the rails 1¼″ wide and cut them 32″ long. Mark them as to their orientation. Cut a ½″-long dovetail in each end. Use each dovetail as a pattern for its mortise, then chop the mortises.

Cut the spacers 4″ wide by 6¾″ long. To maintain grain continuity through the spacers and drawer, cut a spacer from each end of a 32″ piece of stock. Save the center portion for the drawer front.

Next cut the drawer runners, Parts F, 2″ wide. Cut the kicker, Part G, 1¼″ wide. Cut all three pieces 19″ long. Then cut a ¼″ x ¼″ stub tenon on each end.

Cut corresponding mortises in the front apron rails and the rear apron. Rout a continuous groove along the top edge of the rear and side aprons for cabinetmakers' buttons.

Assemble Table

Make a dry assembly, clamping the major pieces. Look for any problems.

Begin the final assembly of the table by gluing the side aprons into the legs. Clamp until dry. Glue the back apron into place and clamp.

Lay the assembly on its back.

Brush glue into the lower dovetailed mortises in the side aprons, and onto the tenons of the drawer runners, Parts F.

Insert the drawer runners into the back apron. Let the runners lean toward the bottom. Now, with the bottom rail in hand, fit the runners and rail together. Then swing the rail into the mortises.

Upright the assembly. Apply glue to the three contact edges of the spacers, Parts C, and put them into place. Brush glue into the upper dovetailed mortises. Seat the top rail, and clamp both rails to the side aprons and the spacers. Bore pilot holes through the rails into the spacers, two at the top and two at the bottom for each spacer. Secure the spacers with 1¼″ x 8 flathead screws.

Apply glue into the mortises for the kicker, Part G. Angle the kicker between the back apron and the front rail and tap it into place.

Bore ³/₁₆″ diameter holes for the tenon. Be sure to stagger the holes in the back legs. Brush a thin layer of glue on the pins and drive them into place.

Cut the top to the given dimensions. Shape the cutout along the front. Use a ½″ round-over bit or some other decorative bit to treat the side and front edges. Leave the back edge square.

CONSTRUCTING THE MIRROR FRAME

Rip the mirror-frame stock 1½″ wide. Cut the rails 16″ and the stiles 24″ long. Cut stub tenons on the rail ends and mortises in the stiles. Be sure to stop the mortises no more than 1½″ into the stiles. Glue up and clamp

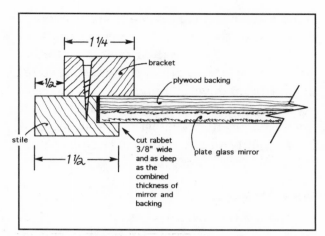

Figure 15.5. Mirror section

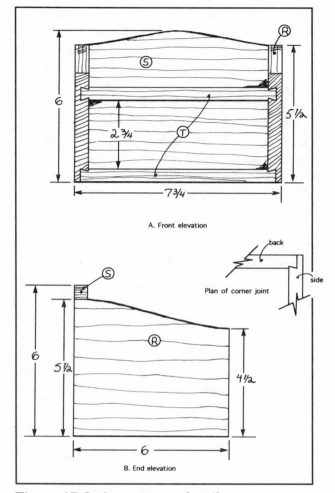

Figure 15.6. Accent tray details

the mirror frame. Check it for square and set it aside to dry thoroughly.

- **Note:** You will rout a ³⁄₈″ rabbet on the back of the frame in which to insert the mirror and backer board. The depth of the rabbet is determined by the combined thickness of the mirror and backer board. Mirror glass comes in ¹⁄₈″ double strength and ¹⁄₄″ plate. Plate glass is recommended because of its strength and its added depth of reflection. The material list indicates a backer board of ¹⁄₄″ plywood. However, ¹⁄₈″ hardboard will work just as well with plate glass. Quarter-inch plywood is the recommended backing for double-strength glass.

Rout the frame to accommodate the mirror and backer board with a ³⁄₈″ rabbet bit with a pilot. It may be necessary to make two or three passes, depending on the desired depth of the cut.

Cut the backer board to fit the frame. Cut the mounting brackets, Parts Q, 1¹⁄₄″ wide and 24″ long. Do not yet mount the glass.

CONSTRUCTING THE ACCENT TRAYS

Assemble the accent trays with sliding-dovetail and dovetailed rabbet joints (Figure 15.6). Select your ¹⁄₂″ stock and rip all the pieces 6″ wide. Cut the shelves, Parts T, and

backs, Parts S, to their finished length of 7¹⁄₄″. Cut the sides, Parts R, about 6¹⁄₂″ long, to be cut to finished length later.

Put a ¹⁄₂″ dovetail bit into the table-mounted router, and set it ¹⁄₄″ above the table. Lay out and cut the dovetailed slots in the sides for the top shelves. Adjust the fence and cut the dovetailed rabbets for the bottom shelves and backs.

Next set the fence to cut the dovetails in the shelf ends. Make enough trial cuts in scrap stock to get the right fit. It should be snug but not so tight that the pieces bind as you slide them together. Adjust the fence to cut the corresponding dovetailed rabbets in the backs and bottom shelves.

Cut the sides to length (6") and rip the shelves 5½" wide. Lay out and cut the curves in the sides and backs according to figure 15.6. Make a dry assembly to determine the best way to apply the clamps.

Working with one assembly at a time, brush glue into the slots of each side, then slide the shelf into place. Apply glue to the rabbets along the back and bottom edges of the sides, and along the back edges of the shelf and of the bottom. Clamp the bottom and back into place. When the glue has set, sand the assemblies thoroughly.

CONSTRUCTING THE DRAWERS

The flush-front main drawer has a ¾"-wide front (cut from the same piece as the spacers) and ½" back and sides. The accent drawers have ½" fronts and backs and ¼" sides. All three drawers are joined with ½" dovetails. Measurements given for the sides assume ¼"-long dovetails. The depth of the

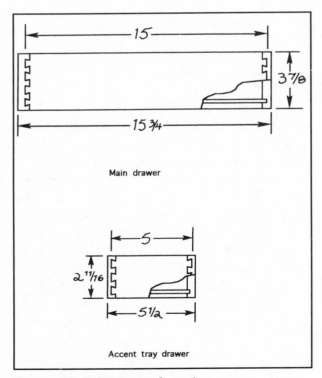

Figure 15.7. Drawer elevations

main drawer can vary since there is enough tolerance in the frame. The accent drawers fit against the back of their openings. Determine the precise length of the sides based on the optimum dovetail length.

How wide to cut the pieces depends on the wood used, its moisture content, and the humidity during construction. Personal judgment is the best guide.

Main Drawer

For the main drawer, re-cut the piece taken from the spacer stock to fit the drawer opening. Cut the back to the same dimensions. Cut the sides accordingly. After cutting the dovetails, cut a ¼"-deep groove in each piece for the bottom. Round over the upper edges of the sides.

Sand the inner surfaces of the pieces before assembling the drawer.

Slide the drawer into its opening and shim it in place with the drawer front flush with the face of the table. Use 1" x 6 flathead screws to secure the drawer guides, Parts H, to the runners. Check the slide of the drawer, and adjust the guides if necessary. Finally, mount a drawer stop at the back.

Accent Drawers

Cut the pieces for the accent drawers to the same dimensions as their openings. After cutting the dovetails, rout a ⅛"-deep groove in all the pieces for the bottoms. Sand the inside surfaces before assembling.

It's likely the drawers will be tight. A sharp block plane and sandpaper will make short work of fitting the drawers perfectly.

FINISHING UP

Do a final sanding with 220-grit paper and finish as you choose.

To mount the top, first drill two countersunk pilot holes in the upper front rail in the extreme ends of the drawer area (next to each spacer).

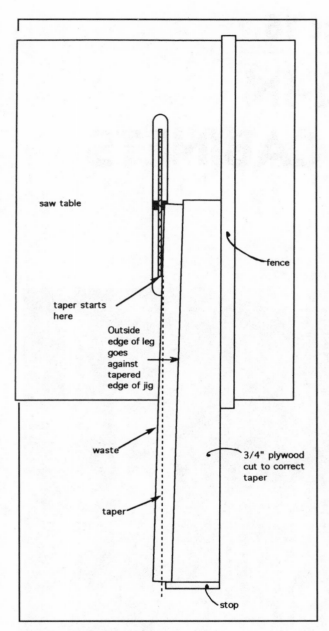

saw table

taper starts
here

Outside
edge of leg
goes
against
tapered
edge of jig

fence

waste

3/4" plywood
cut to correct
taper

taper

stop

Figure 15.8. Taper jig

through the front rail and into the top. Use cabinetmakers' buttons—two on each side apron and at least three along the back—to finish mounting the top.

Lay the mirror frame face down on a clean surface, such as a piece of cardboard or carpet scrap. Set the mirror and backer board into place. Place the brackets, Parts Q, on the back as shown in Figures 15.2 and 15.5.

Bore two countersunk pilot holes through each bracket and into the frame. Be careful not to nick the glass. Secure the bracket to the frame with 1¼" x 6 flathead screws.

Set the mirror upright and centered along the back edge of the table. If necessary, clamp the brackets to the apron while boring two countersunk pilot holes through each bracket and into the apron. Then secure the brackets with four 1¼" x 8 flathead screws.

Next set the trays on either side of the mirror and flush with the back. Drive four 1" x 6 flathead screws from the underside of the top into each tray. Drill pilot holes first. It may be necessary to have someone hold the trays in place during the operation.

Finally, mount the drawer pulls and install the drawers.

• **Hint:** It's easy enough to bore the holes straight through the rail from the top, but how do you countersink them and drive the screws straight in from the bottom? Bore ³/₈" access holes through the bottom rail.

Set the top on the frame, centering it side to side. Make it flush with the back apron. Drive two 1¼" x 8 flathead screws up

▪ Project 16 ▪
BUILT-IN
BEDROOM CABINETS

Take the furniture and other trappings out of an average child's bedroom. What's left are four blank—and probably dingy—walls. Furniture certainly does make the room.

Furniture usually means movable objects used to make a room ready for occu-

pancy. But bedroom furniture *can* be built-in.

Built-in bedroom furniture can not only make an ordinary room special, it can also add value to your home.

I designed and built these built-in bedroom cabinets for a nine-year-old girl. Principal among the many features are a mirrored vanity and a desk with bulletin board. Beneath the desktop are two wide drawers. Above it is a bank of five small drawers. The vanity also has a bank of five drawers. Flanking the vanity mirror are two towers of delicate shelves. Twelve deep drawers, three enclosed cupboards, and three banks of open shelving provide ample storage.

I built and installed the set in two stages: base and upper. Certain design and construction elements reflect the need to be able to assemble the units in the shop, then disassemble them for transport and reassembly.

Built-in furniture is nearly always custom-made for a specific room to suit the needs of the occupants. Therefore, the "how-to" of the bedroom cabinets is a little different from that of the preceding projects. Discussion will be of a general nature. Some measurements are shown in the illustrations and mentioned in the text, but they serve more to give a sense of perspective and reference. The methods of construction can be applied to just about any configuration.

CONSIDERATIONS

Because of the potential for increasing the value of your home, built-in furniture

Figure 16.1. Perspective view

should be made of attractive and durable materials. The bedroom cabinets described here are oak.

Thus far, all the furniture in this book has been made of solid wood, with sparing use of plywood. Because of the large and numerous surfaces appearing in built-in furniture, ³⁄₄″ plywood (or MDF with a hardwood face) is the logical choice for sides and shelves and perhaps tops.

The project presented here makes good use of ³⁄₄″ A2 oak plywood for the sides and shelves. Two-inch-wide solid oak stiles, grooved to fit tongues cut into the plywood, cover the front edges of the sides. The edges of the shelves are banded with a thin strip of oak or faced with part of the framework.

Several of the base units have concealed sides. It isn't necessary to use the more expensive oak plywood; A/C fir works just as well. The same goes for the backs. I used ¹⁄₄″ A3 oak plywood for the backs of the exposed upper units and A/C fir for the backs of the base units.

Individual units are bolted together with 1¹⁄₈″ connector bolts with cap nuts. See the appendix for sources of these mail-order items.

The doors are of frame-and-panel construction, with ¹⁄₄″ plywood used for the panels. The drawer fronts of the base components are solid ³⁄₄″ oak applied to dovetailed drawers made of ¹⁄₂″ pine stock all around. The drawers themselves glide on Accuride Series 1029 center-mount slides.

■ **Note:** The use of a center-mount slide makes its own demands on the drawer's specifications. First, the drawer must have a length that corresponds with one of several mounting holes on the drawer member. Second, to ensure optimum slide performance, the distance between the drawer bottom and the bottom edge of the sides must be ¹⁄₄″. If the distance is greater than ¹⁄₄″, the drawer sides will drag on the plastic tacks

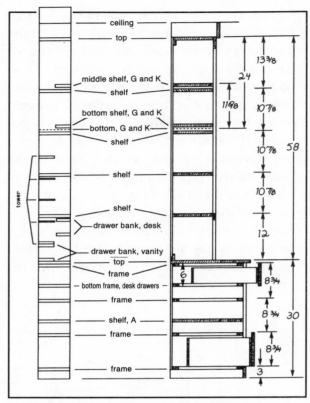

Figure 16.2. Story pole and typical section

supplied with the slide. If the distance is less than ¹⁄₄″, the drawer will wobble.

■ **Note:** Obtain specialized hardware before you begin construction so you don't run into any incompatibility problems.

The top of the desk is made of two pieces of glued-up solid stock, mitered at the corner. The pieces are held together with two ball fasteners, described later. The edges of the top are routed with a ¹⁄₂″ bit with fillet.

PREPARATION

A big project like the built-in bedroom cabinets no doubt seems intimidating at first glance. Actually, it's quite manageable when you break it into individual units.

A set of working drawings is necessary for large projects. The drawings help you to understand the relationship of all the individual pieces. For this project I made three drawings at ³⁄₃₂″ scale and five full-scale drawings. One of the small ones was a plan view showing the placement of the unit in the room. The other two were frontal elevations.

Although the elevations helped me visualize the cabinets, it was the full-scale drawings that I relied on day to day in the shop. I first drew a plan view of each bank of lower, then each bank of upper, components. I lettered the components according to how they would be assembled into the whole.

Next, using a piece of ¼″ plywood 4″ wide and 96″ long, I made a "story pole" to show the elevations of the units and their pieces. The story pole, along with a section drawing for comparison, is shown in Figure 16.2.

CONSTRUCTING THE BASE UNITS

Notice in the inset in Figure 16.3 that the units touch the wall only at their sides, which extend ¼″ beyond the cabinet backs.

This extra ¼″ serves two purposes. First, it allows the cabinet to bridge outward irregularities in the wall. Second, if the wall is out of plumb, you can scribe the cabinet to the wall. Notice also that units A and F don't touch the wall at all, either at the back or the side. This is a precaution against too much plaster build-up in the corner.

Cut the sides of the base units 29¼″ long and, with one exception, 18½″ wide. The exception is the right-hand side of unit A, which is 17¾″, or ¾″ narrower. Mark the sides according to their position in each unit.

Cut a ½″ x ½″ rabbet on the *inside* of the rear edges and a ¼″ x ½″ rabbet on the *outside* of the front edges of each side (but not on the narrow one).

Lay out the frames and, in the case of unit A, the shelves. Cut rabbets in the top edges ¼″ wide by ¾″ deep and dadoes in the field to receive them.

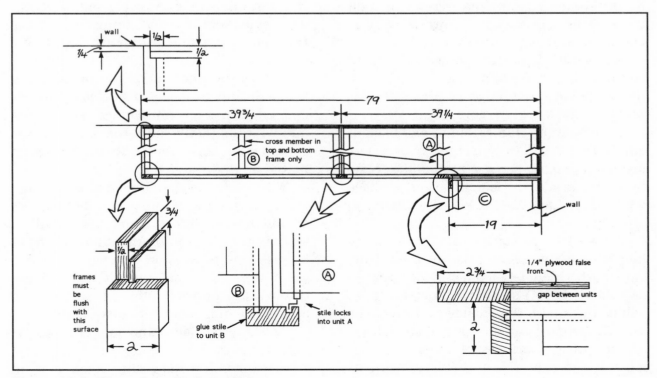

Figure 16.3. Plan of vanity base units

The frames are made of stock ripped 1 1/4″ wide and joined with stub tenons. Glue up the frames, making sure they are square. The front frame rails are oak, but the interior framing members can be of a cheaper wood.

Notice that the base units have a bottom face frame rail but not an upper one.

Rip the stiles 2″ wide. The right-hand stile in unit A is 2 3/4″ wide. Cut them 29 1/4″ long.

As with all furniture, you should check often for square during assembly.

Units A and B

Unit A has one frame at the top and a plywood shelf in the middle and at the bottom. The edge of the bottom shelf is faced with the bottom rail. The middle shelf is edge-banded. Apply the edging before ripping the shelf to width.

Glue the frame and shelves into place. Because both sides are concealed, it makes no difference if you drive screws or nails through the sides to hold the framework in place. Cut and install the back.

▪ **Note:** It's important to make the front edges of all frames and shelves flush with the rabbeted front edge of the sides, as shown in the inset in Figure 16.3.

Assemble the frames, sides, and back of unit B. Do not nail through the exposed side. Instead, drive two screws through the frame from the inside to hold the side in place while the glue sets (as an alternative to clamping).

Notice that in Figure 16.3, each of the four stiles in units A and B is different from one another. The left-hand stile of unit B is dadoed (1/4″ x 1/4″) so that its outside edge will be flush with the outside surface of the side. The right-hand stile is double-dadoed so the outside surfaces of units A and B meet at the center of the stile. The right-hand stile of unit A is 2 3/4″ wide with a

1/4″ x 1/4″ rabbet to hold the false front. The center stile of unit B has no cuts.

▪ **Hint:** Cut the dado for the left-hand (flush) stile 17/32″ from the edge instead of 1/2″. This causes the edge of the stile to protrude slightly beyond the surface of the side. You can then use a cabinet scraper to work the edge perfectly flush with the side. This hint applies to all the stiles intended to be flush with their corresponding sides.

Clamp but do not glue the right- and left-hand stiles to unit B. Now cut and fit the bottom rail between the stiles. You will need a method to make a fast joint. Use a #10 biscuit at each end of the rail to secure it to the stiles. Also use biscuits to secure the center stile to the rail at the bottom and to the top frame rail. Cut and fit the center stile, and lay out its slots. Remove the rail and stiles from the unit.

After you've cut the necessary slots, apply glue to the rabbeted sides of the unit and across the edge of the bottom frame rail. Put one stile into place, and, with biscuits glued and inserted, bring the rail and the remaining end stile into place and clamp.

Now install the center stile. Make sure it is equidistant from the *inside* edge of each end stile. Drive a screw through each of the middle frame rails into the back of the center stile. Make sure the frames aren't bowed up or down.

When unit B is dry, bring it together with unit A on the bench top. The rabbeted side of unit A locks into the end stile of unit B (see inset, Figure 16.3). Align the units flush across their tops, then temporarily clamp them together. Next drill four 3/8″ holes through the units, roughly in each corner. Secure the units with connector bolts.

Lay out the right-hand stile of unit A as shown in Figure 16.3.

Cut the unit A rail slightly long, then cut a slot in the right-hand end and a corresponding slot in the stile for a #10 biscuit. You will also secure the top end of the stile to the top frame rail and the left-hand side of the rail to the bottom shelf with biscuits. Cut those slots now.

Glue and clamp the stile to the face of the unit. Fit the rail between the stiles and glue it into place against the shelf and the right-hand stile (but not against the left-hand stile). Then glue and nail the false front to the unit.

Units C, D, and E

Assemble units C and D in the same way as A and B. Use screws from the inside to secure the frames to the sides.

Use solid stock or plywood for the sides of unit E. It is not necessary to rabbet the back into the sides, so you should cut the sides as long as the frames are wide. Rabbet the top and bottom edges $1/4'' \times 3/4''$ to receive the frames.

Glue and screw the sides to the frames, then tack on the back. Use #10 biscuits to anchor the center stile to the frames.

Clamp unit E between C and D. Secure the units with two connector bolts on each side of unit E.

Now bring assembly A–B together with C–D–E. Join them with two connector bolts at the front of unit C. Notice the gap between the two assemblies at the back (Figure 16.3). This allows for some flexibility during final assembly. For now, shim the cabinets so they are square at the front.

Drill a series of holes across the front frame rails and slotted holes along the side and back frame rails for mounting the top.

Top

Make the top from glued-up solid stock. Working with long boards is a challenge, but the results are rewarding. Give the blanks some extra width and as much as six extra inches of length, in case you have to fiddle with the miter. The finished top should hang over the cabinets by about 1″ at the front and ends.

Once the blanks are dry, work them smooth and flat. Rip them to width. Then cut their miters. If you use a circular saw, remember to cut from the bottom and to use a guide. Lay the sections on the assembled base units, making sure the front edges are parallel, and check the fit. Chances are the miter will need some work. Take down slight discrepancies with a block plane. For greater errors, use a router chucked with a straight bit or flush trim bit against a guide or template clamped to the blanks.

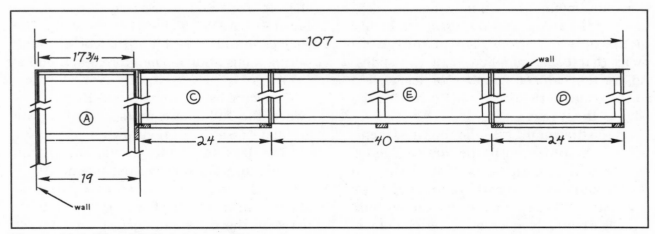

Figure 16.4. Plan of desk base units

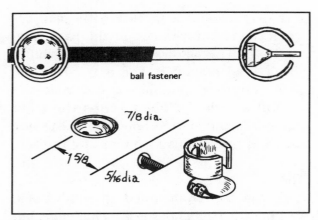

Figure 16.5. Top joinery detail

Join the top sections with two ball fasteners (Figure 16.5). You will need a ⁷⁄₈″ Forstner bit to bore the ⁵⁄₈″-deep, flat-bottomed holes. Tighten the fasteners and again check the fit of the miter.

Align the top with the cabinets, mark the ends, and cut the sections to length. Finally, rout a decorative edge into the top.

Drawers

The base drawers have oak fronts applied to pine boxes joined with dovetails front and back. You may, of course, use a different material inside or a different joinery method. Fit all the drawers before applying the fronts.

Following the instructions enclosed with the slide, mount the cabinet member centered in the frame and the drawer member to the drawer bottom. Tap in the plastic tacks that come supplied with the slides. Adjust the cabinet member of each slide so the front of the drawer is flush with the edge of the frame.

If the drawer drags, shim the fixed member of the slide until the drawer glides evenly on the plastic tacks. If the clearance is right and the drawer still wobbles, there is probably a "belly" in the drawer bottom, which effectively decreases the clearance. You will need to rout (with a table-mounted

³⁄₄″ straight bit) or scrape a channel in the drawer bottom to make a level bed for the slide.

Cut the applied fronts so there is no more than ¹⁄₁₆″ clearance on each side. For an added touch, cut the fronts for units B and E in pairs from the same board so the grain matches. Then rout a ³⁄₁₆″ cove around the perimeter. This adds visual interest and disguises minor discrepancies in the margin.

With the drawer in place, tightly shim the applied front in the opening. Drive four 1″ x 8 flathead screws through the inside of the drawer front into the applied front.

To install the drawer pulls with the supplied screws, you'll need to counterbore the holes into the drawer front from the inside.

CONSTRUCTING THE UPPER UNITS

The upper units are built in much the same way as the lower. The sides are 11½″ wide and have the same rabbet cuts front and back. The right-hand side of unit F is 10¾″, as are the tops and fixed shelves of all the units. Units F, H, I, and J run from the countertop to four inches or so below the ceiling (58″ tall in this case). A valance fills the gap between the top of the cabinets and the ceiling.

The units on either side of the desk feature three adjustable shelves. The bottom shelves are fixed to add rigidity and are faced with a 1¼″ rail between the stiles. The shelves in unit F reach to the corner, hampering adjustability. Therefore, each one is fixed.

The cupboards, units G and K, hang between the full-length units on either side and have no stiles of their own.

The desk and vanity insets, units L and M, slip into place during final assembly.

All the upper units except H need an anchor rail at the top. The 1¼″-wide rail fits between the sides and against the back. It requires no special cuts.

The open shelf units need an anchor rail at the bottom, which also supports the back (Figure 16.2). The inset in Figure 16.6 illustrates the rabbet cuts needed in the 1¼" rail. Round over the rail's upper edge with a ¼" bit.

Unit F

Cut the ¼" x ¾" rabbets and dadoes in the sides for the top and shelves. The top and

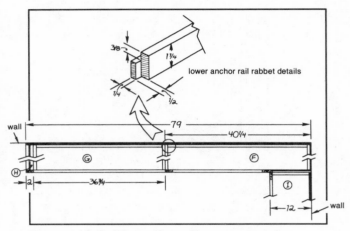

Figure 16.6. Plan of vanity upper units

bottom shelves are faced with rails. The three middle shelves are edge-banded. Band them their full length, then rip them the same width as the top and bottom.

Glue in the shelves and clamp them in place. Glue and clamp the upper anchor rail to the underside of the top. Apply glue to the ends of the lower anchor rail, and tack it into place at the bottom.

Place the unit on its back. Cut the 3" upper rail and 1¼" lower rail to length. Then cut slots in the ends of the upper rail and in the stiles for a #10 biscuit.

Glue the left-hand stile into place and clamp. When dry, glue in the rails and the right-hand stile. Before clamping anything in place, use a straightedge across the bottom to check the vertical placement of the right-hand stile. It must line up exactly with

the sides. Clamp everything into place, and recheck the center stile. Then glue and tack down the false front. Turn the unit over and secure the back.

Units I and J

Units I and J are simple cases with a top, a fixed bottom shelf, and three adjustable shelves between. They are the same but for width. The sides of each require the stan-

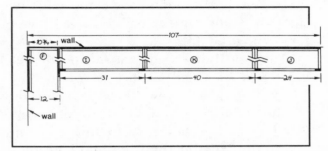

Figure 16.7. Plan of upper desk units

dard rabbet cuts front and back. The front top rails are plate-joined to their stiles.

Lay out and cut the rabbets and dadoes for the top and bottom shelves. Next lay out and bore holes for the shelf pins. I used 4mm brass pins, but any style will do. I placed the holes about 8" from the top and bottom (above the bottom shelf), 1" in from the front and back, and 1½" apart. Take care to space them evenly.

Glue the tops and fixed shelves into place, then the upper and lower anchor rails. Next glue on the back. Turn the unit over. Fit one stile, the top rail, then the other stile in one operation. Clamp them into place, and apply the bottom front rail.

Unit H

Unit H is nothing more than a wide end post. As shown in Figure 16.6, it is made of two rabbeted sides held at the front by a single stile and at the back by a strip of ¼" plywood.

Units G and K

The cupboard units, G and K, are the same but for width. The shelves are the same width as the sides, 10¾″. Band the edges of the shelves and sides before ripping them to width. Cut a typical rabbet in the top edges of the sides. The bottom shelf rests in dadoes cut ½″ up from the bottom edge of the sides. Glue up the pieces and secure with screws. Then tack on the back.

The cupboard units have no stiles of their own, but they do have a top rail. For the best results, pre-assemble the units before fitting the rails.

Lay unit H on its side, outside down. Set unit G in its place against it. Drive four 1½″ x 10 flathead screws through the inside of the cabinet into unit H. Upend this assembly and place it next to unit F. Clamp one to the other at the front and bore four ⅜″ holes, roughly in the corners, through both units at the same time. Use a backer board to prevent the bit from tearing through the other side. Fasten the two assemblies with 1⅛″ connector bolts and cap nuts.

Assemble units I, J, and K with four connector bolts in each side of unit K. Be careful not to let the connector bolts interfere with the pin holes for the adjustable shelves.

Bring the two assemblies together, and join them with two connector bolts at the front. Like the base units, there is a gap between the adjacent units at the back.

Now fit and install the rails for cupboard units.

Doors

Now that the cabinets are assembled, you can accurately measure, build, and fit the doors (as well as the door for unit A). They are simple frame-and-panel construction, as shown in Figure 16.8.

If the ¼″ plywood you've chosen for

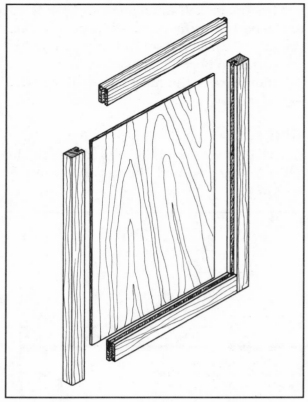

Figure 16.8. Typical frame-and-panel door

the door panels has book-matched plies on the face, careful cutting will yield book-matched doors, as shown in the photograph.

Rip the rails and stiles 2″ wide. Cut all the pieces to rough length, and prepare to groove them for the panel.

Lay all the pieces on the bench in order. Mark their outside faces and the edges to be grooved.

The fastest way to cut the ¼″-deep grooves is by making two passes on a table saw, one with either face against the fence. This automatically centers the groove. It also allows for a fine adjustment of the width of the groove to match the thickness of the plywood.

Cut the rails to their exact length, *including* the tenons. Cut the stiles ¼″ longer than necessary.

Glue the rails to the panel first. Brush glue on the tenons, then clamp the stiles to the assembled rails and panel. Check each door for square before the glue sets. Then carefully trim off the ''ears'' at each end of the stiles.

Valance

The valance closes the gap between the cabinets and ceiling. It has three elements, as shown in Figure 16.9: main board, mounting board, and trim.

Cut the main board wide enough that it comes down the face of the cabinet about ¹⁄₂″ but clears the ceiling by about ¹⁄₄″. The mounting board is glued and screwed to the back of the main board ¹⁄₂″ up from the bottom.

Cut each of the main boards a little long to have enough to achieve a good miter around the outside corners. The inside corner is a butt joint, so run the longer board all the way into the corner and let the adjacent board butt into it.

CONSTRUCTING THE VANITY AND DESK INSETS

The insets, units L and M, have the common element of a bank of five drawers. Although the banks—and drawers—are different widths, the drawers are the same height and depth. There are two other differences. The obvious one is that the desk drawers are elevated. This changes the profile of each (Figure 16.10C-D). The edging of the countertop is duplicated in the top edges of both the desk and vanity drawer cases. The bottom edge of the desk case is edged as well, but the vanity case is square since it sits directly on the countertop.

The less obvious difference is in the case backs. The desk case is mounted directly to the bulletin board and has no back of its own. The vanity case, on the other hand, does have a back with the dual functions of stopping the drawers and supporting the mirror (Figure 16.10C).

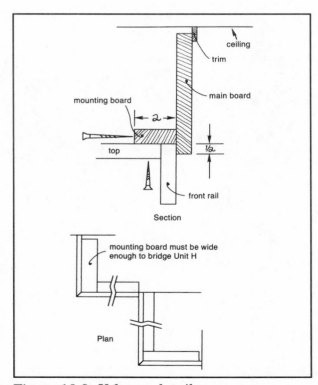

Figure 16.9. Valance details

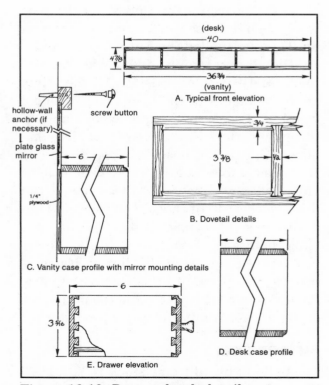

Figure 16.10. Drawer bank details

The top edge of the mirror is held in place with $^3/_4'' \times 1^1/_4''$ strip, rabbeted the depth of the mirror (Figure 16.10C). Predrill three evenly spaced holes and counterbore them for $^3/_8''$ screw buttons.

Drawer Banks

The tops and bottoms of the cases are made of $^3/_4''$ stock ripped 6" wide. The sides and dividers are $^1/_2''$ thick and $3^7/_8''$ wide by 6" long. Lay out and cut $^1/_2''$ dovetailed slots $^1/_4''$ deep for the dividers (Figure 16.10B). Be sure to use a backer block at the end of the cuts to guard against tear-out.

For the dividers, make enough test cuts in scrap stock to ensure a good fit. The pieces should slide into place smoothly with as little play as possible, but should not be so tight that they bind. Dovetail the end pieces on the insides only.

Working quickly, apply glue to the dovetails and slip them into place top and bottom. Make sure the front edges are flush.

Cut the back for the vanity case $^1/_4''$ narrower than the case itself, but don't put it on until you've applied the finish to the case.

The drawer fronts and backs are $^1/_2''$ thick, and the sides are $^1/_4''$. All the joints are dovetailed. Cut the fronts from a single board, and mark their sequence to maintain the grain pattern. Cut the pieces to the same dimensions as the inside of the case. Once you've assembled the drawers, fit them individually. Leave about $^1/_{16}''$ clearance at the top and sides. To fit them front to back, hold a piece of scrap against the back of the case. Slide the drawer in until it stops. Plane off portions of the back of the drawer, if necessary, so the front fits flush with the case. Finally, rout a $^1/_8''$ cove around the perimeter of the drawer fronts and apply the pulls.

Bulletin Board

The bulletin board frame stock is $^3/_4'' \times 1^1/_4''$. The stiles are stub-tenoned into the rails,

which run the full length between the shelf units. The bulletin board itself is made of cork glued to a $^1/_4''$ plywood backing. You can purchase cork off a roll or in squares.

Before you glue the cork to the backing, determine the combined thickness of the two and rout a $^3/_8''$-wide rabbet on the back of the frame. Next cut the backing board and check the fit. Round the corners to fit the arc left by the router on the frame's inside corners.

Place the frame face up on the bench and mark the position of the drawer case, 6" up from the bottom. Use a radial-arm saw to recess the frame to the depth of the rabbet (Figure 16.11).

Thin an amount of wood glue with a little water, and liberally coat the backing board. (Contact cement or mastic will work

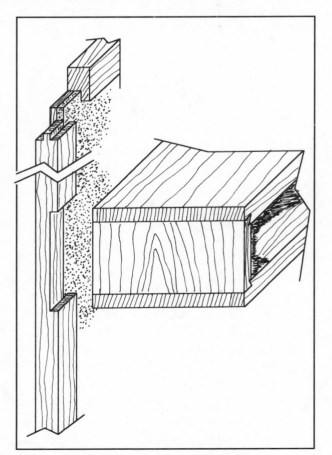

Figure 16.11. Bulletin board detail

as well.) Place the cork to the backing board, and apply even weight until dry. Let the cork run by the edges of the backing board. They can be trimmed later.

The bulletin board will be secured to the wall with screws. Predrill the holes now and counterbore them for ³⁄₈″ screw buttons. Space the holes evenly about 12″ apart.

▪ **Note:** The bulletin board supports the weight of the drawers and their contents. Therefore, the unit must be mounted securely.

When you've applied the finish to the frame and drawer case, mount the cork board in the frame. Small flathead screws work well. Next place the drawer case face down on the bench. Then place the bulletin board on the case, aligning the case in the recess in the frame. Drive 1¼″ x 8 flathead screws through the back into the case, spacing them 6″ apart along the top and bottom.

Towers

The two towers that flank the mirror add an elegant touch. They have no backs, so the mirror reflects through them. Their sweeping concave shape draws the eye to the center of the vanity unit.

The sides, top, and bottom are ½″ thick and half-dovetailed together. The ¼″ shelves slide into ³⁄₁₆″-deep dadoes (Figure 16.12).

Rip the outer sides 5″ wide and the inner sides 3″ wide. Cut the tops and bottoms 5″ square to begin with. Cut the dovetails and test the fit. Then cut the arcs according to the pattern in Figure 16.12. Smooth them out, taking care not to make them too short where they meet the inner sides.

Next lay out and cut the dadoes for the shelves. Glue up the sides, top, and bottom.

Cut the shelves square and test their fit. They should slide in and out easily. (You won't glue them in; leaving them loose will

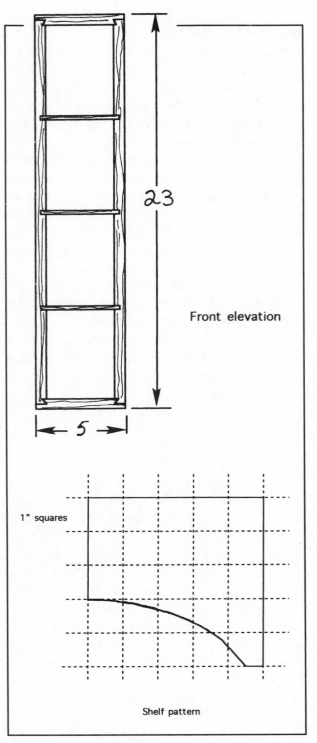

Figure 16.12. Vanity tower detail

facilitate cleaning the mirror.) Trace the pattern onto the shelves and cut the arcs.

INSTALLATION

The built-in bedroom cabinets should be installed on a bare floor. If the room where they will be installed is carpeted, you will need to remove the carpet, pad, and tack strip. In any case remove the baseboard. Use the base cabinets as a template.

Also note the location of any electrical outlets that might be covered up. Consider relocating outlets above the countertop by cutting a hole in the back of the upper cabinet and bringing the outlet forward. Trim the outlet with an oak plate. For an extra charge, your mirror supplier will cut an opening for an outlet in the glass itself.

▪ **Note:** Most local building codes require that all junction boxes be accessible. If any of the cabinets cover an outlet, it must be made accessible—even if it's behind a drawer. Cut any necessary access holes in the cabinet backs.

▪ **Note:** For any questions regarding wiring, consult a qualified electrician.

Bring units A and B into place and bolt them together. Check the fit of the left side of unit A against the wall. (Make sure the unit is plumb.) Scribe it to the wall if necessary. Bolt unit E between C and D, then check the fit against the wall. Join both assemblies at the corner. Check that the works are level; plumb and shim where necessary.

Locate the studs in the wall. Predrill and counterbore holes in the back frame rail. Use shims to take up the space between the cabinet back and the wall. Then anchor the cabinet to the wall using screws of sufficient length. Transfer the stud locations to the top of the wall for reference later.

Tack the carpet to the floor around the perimeter of the cabinets. Cut the baseboard as necessary and reinstall.

Bring the countertop sections into place, and join them with the ball fasteners. Check the overall fit. The only place the top needs to be tight to the wall is at the extreme ends. Other gaps will be concealed by the upper

units. With the top in place, fasten it to the top frame with $1\frac{1}{4}'' \times 8$ flathead screws driven up through the frames.

Set unit F in place on the countertop. Screw unit G to unit H, then bolt G to F. Bolt together units I, J, and K. Then join the two assemblies at the corner.

Check that everything is in alignment, then drive finish screws—black screws with smaller heads—through the top and bottom anchor rails. Fit shims over the top and behind the upper anchor rail. You won't be able to shim the bottom rail; just drive the screws snug. Avoid bowing the back of the cabinet. Hang the doors and install their pulls and magnetic catches.

Place the bulletin board assembly where it belongs and mark the screw holes on the wall. Remove the assembly and install any necessary hollow-wall fasteners. Replace the unit, anchor with screws, and cap the screws with screw buttons.

Slide the vanity drawer case into place. Locate two studs behind it and drive two screws through the back of the case into the studs. Make sure unit H is firmly against the wall, then drive a screw through the inside of the drawer case into unit H.

Tip in the mirror, letting it rest on the back of the drawer case. (See Figure 16.10C.) Have an assistant hold it in place while you use the top anchor strip to mark the positions of the hollow-wall anchors. Install the anchors, then screw the anchor strip to the wall. Cap the holes with screw buttons. Set the vanity towers in place and secure with brads tacked through the bottom and through the sides. Countersink the brads and fill the holes with putty.

Finally, install the valance. Set the longest piece—the one that runs all the way into the corner—into place, and check the fit. When it's to your liking, drive $1\frac{1}{2}''$ screws up through the top of the cabinet as shown in Figure 16.9. Install the second piece in the same way. Then tack on the trim strip.